Library of
Davidson College

Policy Papers in International Affairs

NUMBER 25

Reassessing the Soviet Challenge in Africa

Michael Clough EDITOR

CONTRIBUTORS: Paul B. Henze · Martin Lowenkopf · John Marcum

FOREWORD BY Robert M. Price

Institute of International Studies
UNIVERSITY OF CALIFORNIA · BERKELEY

$8.00

INSTITUTE OF INTERNATIONAL STUDIES
UNIVERSITY OF CALIFORNIA, BERKELEY

CARL G. ROSBERG
Director

NEIL J. SMELSER
Associate Director

HARRY KREISLER
Assistant Director

The Institute of International Studies was established at the University of California, Berkeley, in 1955. Its major purpose for the past two decades has been to promote interdisciplinary research and training in comparative/international and policy-related studies. The major components of the Institute's program are: *Research*, which ranges from individual investigations by faculty members to large-scale projects involving many faculty and student researchers; *Colloquia*, which bring together faculty, graduate students, visiting scholars, and public and private policymakers to pursue inquiries into special areas of interest, such as U. S. foreign policy, international political economy, national and international science policy, problems of twentieth-century capitalism, comparative methodology in the social sciences, comparative communism, and demography; *Lecture Series*, which consists of lecture-discussion meetings at which policymakers and specialists from the U. S., foreign, and international governments and agencies, journalists, and visiting U. S. and foreign scholars present their views to assemblages of interested faculty and students; *Publications*, through which Institute-related research is made available in book-length monographs and policy papers; *Teaching and Student Programs*, through which the Institute sponsors undergraduate interdisciplinary majors related to the international/comparative focus of the Institute and provides supplementary support for qualified Ph.D. candidates completing their dissertations; *Conference and Visiting Scholars Program*, through which the Institute sponsors conferences on major issues of international concern and academic interest and provides administrative support for senior scholars and policymakers who are appointed Visiting Fellows; and *Library*, in which the Institute maintains a specialized collection of more than 11,000 books and 10,000 periodicals and pamphlets.

Elements of the Institute's program are carried on in conjunction with the several area centers on the Berkeley campus dealing with African, Chinese, Japanese and Korean, Latin American, Middle Eastern, Slavic and East European, and South and Southeast Asian studies. The Institute also collaborates with other organizations—both on and off campus—in efforts to increase public understanding of issues in international affairs confronting the U. S. and the world.

Policy Papers
in International Affairs
NUMBER 25

Reassessing the Soviet Challenge in Africa

Michael Clough EDITOR

CONTRIBUTORS: Paul B. Henze
Martin Lowenkopf · John Marcum

FOREWORD BY Robert M. Price

Institute of
International Studies
UNIVERSITY OF CALIFORNIA • BERKELEY

In sponsoring the Policy Papers in International Affairs series, the Institute of International Studies reasserts its commitment to a vigorous policy debate by providing a forum for innovative approaches to important policy issues. The views expressed in each paper are those of the author only, and publication in this series does not constitute endorsement by the Institute.

International Standard Book Number 0-87725-525-3

Library of Congress Catalog Card Number 86-81139

© 1986 by the Regents of the University of California

CONTENTS

Foreword: U.S.-Soviet Relations in Regional Environments
ROBERT M. PRICE vii

Notes on Contributors xi

INTRODUCTION
Michael Clough with Donald Jordan 1

BIPOLAR DEPENDENCY: THE PEOPLE'S REPUBLIC OF ANGOLA
John Marcum 12

MARXISM-LENINISM IN ETHIOPIA: POLITICAL IMPASSE AND ECONOMIC DETERIORATION
Paul B. Henze 31

MOZAMBIQUE: THE NKOMATI ACCORD
Martin Lowenkopf 48

CONCLUSION: COMING TO TERMS WITH RADICAL SOCIALISM
Michael Clough 69

Appendix: The Nkomati Accord 91

Bibliography 97

FOREWORD

U.S.-SOVIET RELATIONS IN REGIONAL ENVIRONMENTS

Robert M. Price

In the contemporary world three dimensions of politics which are usually analyzed separately—superpower relations, regional politics, and domestic political processes—are continuously intermeshed. If one scans the geographic zones of superpower contention, this fact is strikingly revealed. In the Middle East and Persian Gulf, in Central America, in South and Southeast Asia, in Europe, and in southern Africa and the Horn, the United States and the Soviet Union do not contend with each other directly, but rather through a filter of local and regional affairs. The relationship between the two superpowers is affected by, and affects, the politics of each region. In turn, the domestic politics of local states are closely coupled to regional dynamics, and thus directly or indirectly to the U.S.-Soviet relationship as well. Consequently, U.S. or Soviet actions have complex local and regional ramifications. These complicate and constrain the policies of both superpowers, their relationship with each other, their role in various geopolitical regions, and their bilateral relations with third countries.

Things were not always this way. For at least two decades after the end of World War II, the United States could pursue its global role vis-à-vis the Soviet Union free for the most part of the constraining effects of regional and domestic political dynamics in Europe, Latin America, Asia, and Africa. Ultimately this was the operational meaning of the concept of "free-world leadership." For better or worse, the structural conditions that provided the basis for this leadership no longer pertain. Europe and Japan have fully recovered from the devastation of World War II, Asia and Africa have emerged from colonial status, and significant parts of Latin America have attained considerable economic development. The result, as most observers of global affairs recognize, has been a new assertiveness: many countries that previously would willingly follow U.S. "leadership" now insist on defining their own national interests and acting on them irrespective of U.S. desires. In other words, in the last decade and a half the international system has become more diffuse and pluralistic, and this new structure of power is reflected in the intermingling of great power, regional, and local political relationships that is so evident today.

This situation both confounds Washington's and Moscow's task of fashioning feasible policy and invests regional policies with increased importance. To the extent that policymakers in the United States (or Soviet Union) approach the world with a cognitive framework that is essentially bipolar, they will fail to comprehend the nature of the regional "prism" through which the two countries interact and contend. Consequently, they are likely to exaggerate both their own and their adversary's capacity to affect outcomes; to miscalculate the nature of perceived threats; and to be insensitive to the local and regional ramifications of their policies and to the unintended effects these can have on their nation's long-term interests.

It is certainly true that in the United States policymakers have since the Vietnam War at least verbally recognized the more pluralistic character of contemporary world politics, but they have continued to operate with the bipolar, Soviet-threat-dominated cognitive framework that has guided U.S. policy since the close of World War II. This can be most clearly observed in the assessment of the significance of Soviet involvements in regional affairs. During the past forty years the foreign policy community in the United States (officials, journalists, opinion leaders, and scholars) has operated with a conception of contemporary global politics which assumes a priori that such Soviet involvements have a zero-sum significance for the United States, and such a conception still dominates American thinking. Soviet gains are assumed to entail American losses. U.S. foreign policy is invariably justified, in the final analysis, as serving to stem (or sometimes turn back) the "flow" of Soviet influence or presence.

When policymakers within two relatively equally matched and globally oriented superpowers assume their relations with each other are zero-sum, international politics will inevitably move in a precarious, tension-oriented, and conflict-generating direction. This is built into the very assumption which guides policy. Here lies the underlying dynamic pushing in the direction of U.S.-Soviet conflict.

In contrast, if policymakers approached the world with a very different set of assumptions, ones that allowed for situations of non-zero-sum relations between the United States and USSR, then the potential for conflict would be substantially reduced. Perhaps such an approach is impossible because the zero-sum assumption reflects the reality of Soviet intentions and actions. But this reality is too important a matter to be left to assumption. The zero-sum conception ought to be demonstrable or discarded. More precisely, it is important that thinking and research be directed toward distinguishing those types of situations in which Soviet interests and actions imply a zero-sum relationship with the United States from those that do not. Such thinking, however, demands new ways of looking at the world; it requires recognizing that in the contemporary world the local and regional contexts within which the superpowers usually contend are prisms which significantly shape what each power can and will do and what the consequences of their actions will be.

The diffuse nature of contemporary world power not only confounds the making of feasible foreign policy, but also complicates understanding and analysis. It has been characteristic of the U.S. analytic community to study U.S.-Soviet relations as an aspect of U.S. national security or strategic studies. This is of course reflective of the postwar view of global power as highly concentrated in the country that represented and guaranteed the interests of an essentially homogeneous "free world." Rarely was expertise on the Soviet Union viewed as important to an understanding of the relations between the world's two most powerful states. Since the USSR was presumed to have no "legitimate" interests in the free world and since the objective of policy was to deny the Soviets the power to pursue other types of interests, little premium was placed on a nuanced understanding of Soviet views of their foreign interests and priorities. During the 1970s, as the Soviet Union approached a rough military parity with the United States and thus became capable of projecting its power globally, the need for such understanding has become ever clearer. Consequently, in recent years attention has been given to training scholars whose main expertise will be Soviet foreign policy. The Rockefeller Foundation's funding for Programs on Soviet International Behavior is one manifestation of this new tendency.

However important the need to upgrade our expertise on Soviet foreign policy interests and processes, the contemporary intermeshing of global, regional, and local dimensions of politics requires more in the way of analytic breadth. It requires combining knowledge about U.S. and Soviet foreign policy with expertise about the regional and local political arenas in which U.S. and Soviet policy engage because these arenas have an independent effect upon the superpower relationship. The contributions to this volume situate U.S.-Soviet relations in one geographic region—sub-Saharan Africa.

In respect to East-West interaction, two contrasting tendencies mark the sub-Saharan Africa arena. On the one hand, although prior to the late 1950s neither the United States nor Soviet Union had a major presence south of the Sahara, the political turmoil that has marked the first decades of independence has provided ample opportunity for both superpowers to expand their influence. Processes of economic disintegration and political deterioration within African states are usually viewed in the United States as providing an opening for the Soviets, and thus a need for America to take preemptive or reactive countermeasures. On the other hand, sub-Saharan Africa is the only world region not within the post-World War II system of security treaties. Consequently, when competition and contention have occurred—as during the Congo Crisis of 1960-61, and more recently in the Horn and southern Africa—they have been without the historical legacy of claims to zones of exclusive influence and vital interest on the part of either the Soviet Union or the United States. As a result, although a likely arena for superpower opportunity and thus potential contention, sub-Saharan Africa may also be the region in which it will be easiest to work out modes of superpower crisis prevention, and in which a non-zero-sum relationship between the United States and USSR might evolve. As such, sub-Saharan Africa can serve as a unique laboratory for the study of U.S.-Soviet interaction.

NOTES ON CONTRIBUTORS

MICHAEL CLOUGH is Assistant Professor of Political Science at the University of Wisconsin-Madison.

PAUL B. HENZE is a Resident Consultant at the Rand Corporation, Washington, D.C.

MARTIN LOWENKOPF is with the U.S. Department of State. He was on leave in 1984-85 and taught at the School of Advanced International Studies, Johns Hopkins University.

JOHN MARCUM is Professor of Politics at the University of California, Santa Cruz.

ROBERT M. PRICE is Associate Professor of Political Science at the University of California, Berkeley.

DONALD JORDAN is a lecturer in political science at the U.S. Air Force Academy, Colorado Springs.

INTRODUCTION

Michael Clough with Donald Jordan

The mid-1970s are widely believed to have marked a watershed for the Soviet Union—and by implication the United States—in Africa. "The massive Soviet-Cuban intervention into the Angolan civil war in 1975," wrote Thomas Henriksen, "opened a new chapter in the Soviet Union's relations with African states, as well as heralding a bold and aggressive foreign policy on the world stage" (1983:263). In the judgment of Gerard Chaliand, the successful Soviet interventions in Angola and then Ethiopia in 1977 signaled the end of a "period when Africa was a Western preserve" (1982:40). This turn of events caught most Western analysts and policymakers by surprise. It touched off an intense debate over the nature of the Soviet "threat" in Africa and caused the United States to adopt a much more activist policy toward the continent.

Two unanticipated and unrelated events in 1974 set in motion a series of developments that changed superpower perceptions of Africa's geopolitical importance. First, in April 1974 the Movimento das Forças Armadas (MFA), a group of officers radicalized by their experiences in Portugal's colonial wars, seized power in Lisbon and began the process of granting independence to Angola, Cape Verde, Guinea-Bissau, Mozambique, and São Tomé and Principe. Negotiated agreements between the Portuguese government and the predominant nationalist party in each territory resulted in largely uncontested transfers of power everywhere except Angola. There a long-standing three-way rivalry among the Movimento Popular de Libertação de Angola (MPLA), led by Agostinho Neto, the Frente Nacional de Libertação de Angola (FNLA), led by Holden Roberto, and the União Nacional para a Independência Total de Angola (UNITA), led by Jonas Savimbi, quickly escalated into a civil war.*

---

*The definitive history of the Angolan revolution is Marcum (1969/1978). Two other useful studies are Klinghoffer (1980) and Ebinger (1984).

Second, in September 1974 another group of radical officers ousted an aged and besieged Emperor Haile Selassie in Ethiopia and formed a ruling committee, which came to be known as the Derg, to chart a revolutionary course for Ethiopia. Bitter, bloody power struggles ensued, both among rival factions within the Derg and between the Derg and a host of challengers throughout the country. Sensing an opportunity to seize control of the Ogaden province, in 1977 neighboring Somalia invaded Ethiopia.*

In the Angolan civil war Soviet equipment and Cuban troops enabled the MPLA to defeat a military challenge from a force comprised of units from the FNLA, UNITA, Zaire, South Africa, and a breakaway faction of the MPLA led by Daniel Chipenda.† Following its victory, the MPLA moved to translate its ideological commitment to socialism into practice. In October 1976 a meeting of the MPLA Central Committee adopted "scientific socialism—Marxism-Leninism" as its official doctrine, and in December 1977, at its first party congress, the MPLA formally converted itself into a vanguard Marxist-Leninist "labor party." The MPLA's alliance with the Soviet Union was solidified in October 1976 by the signing of a Treaty of Friendship and Cooperation which provided for cooperation in all fields, including military. Angola has "opted for socialism," President Neto declared in December 1977, and "this option of ours determines our positions and our relations with the socialist states" (quoted in Rothenberg 1980:124).**

Ethiopia's conflicts produced a similar outcome, albeit through a very different process. An Ethiopian-Soviet alliance of sorts was formed following the emergence of Mengistu Haile Mariam as the dominant figure in the Derg in February 1977 and the Somali invasion a few months later. After an attempt by Fidel Castro to arrange a "fraternal" agreement among the "socialist" states and movements of Ethiopia, Somalia, and Eritrea failed, the Soviet Union and Cuba threw their support behind Mengistu. Once again

---

*On the Ethiopian revolution, see Ottaway and Ottaway (1978), Halliday and Molyneux (1981), and Henze (1981). On the history of conflict in the Horn of Africa, see Farer (1979), M. Ottaway (1982), and Selassie (1980).

†On Soviet intervention in Angola, see Legum (1976), Porter (1984:147-81), Garthoff (1985:502-37), and Valenta (1980). On Cuban intervention in Angola, see LeoGrande (1980), Durch (1978), and Henriksen (1983).

**On the consolidation of socialism in Angola after independence, see Ottaway and Ottaway (1981:99-127) and Zafris (1982).

Soviet equipment and Cuban material proved decisive.* By February 1978 Somalia was forced to withdraw, and the Derg began to reimpose its control by force in Eritrea. Formal ties with the socialist bloc developed quickly. On 20 November 1978 Ethiopia signed a Treaty of Friendship and Cooperation with the Soviet Union. But Mengistu resisted Soviet and Cuban pressures to form a civilian vanguard party. Although he embraced "scientific socialism" as early as April 1976, a Commission for Organizing the Party of the Working People of Ethiopia (COPWE) was not formed until December 1979. Almost five more years were to pass before the Ethiopian Workers' Party came into being.†

Developments in Mozambique reinforced the perception that a new wave of radical socialism was building in Africa. The Frente de Libertação de Moçambique (FRELIMO), led by Samora Machel, assumed power in July 1975.** During its liberation struggle, FRELIMO had maintained a balanced relationship with the Soviet Union and China; unlike the MPLA, FRELIMO was not forced to rely on outside intervention to gain power. Once in power, however, Machel and his supporters decided that a close relationship with the Soviet Union was essential to their survival. On 31 March 1977 Mozambique signed a Treaty of Friendship and Cooperation with the Soviet Union. Machel soon became one of the most vocal proponents of the view that the Soviet Union constituted a "natural ally" of the Third World. Internally, FRELIMO lost no time in choosing the socialist path. At its Third Party Congress in April 1977, FRELIMO's leaders unequivocally rejected "African socialism" in favor of "scientific socialism" and began to reorganize FRELIMO as a vanguard party.††

The pattern of change in Angola, Ethiopia, and Mozambique was widely interpreted as a watershed in Soviet relations with the Third World for two reasons. First, the interventions in Angola and

---

*On Soviet intervention in the Horn, see Porter (1984:182-215), Garthoff (1985:630-53), and Henze (1983a).

†On the development of socialism in Ethiopia, see Henze (1985), Keller (1985), Ottaway and Ottaway (1981:128-56), and Funk (1985).

**On the history of the Mozambican revolution, see Isaacman and Isaacman (1983a), Henriksen (1979), and Munslow (1983).

††On the consolidation of socialism in Mozambique after independence, see Ottaway and Ottaway (1981:68-98), Campbell (1984), Kuhne (1985), Hanlon (1984), and Saul (1985).

Ethiopia, and the continuing commitments contained in the Treaties of Friendship and Cooperation, substantiated Moscow's claims to full superpower status. "Today," Leonid Brezhnev declared in 1970, "no question of any importance in the world can be decided without our participation and without consideration of our economic and military might" (quoted in Rothenberg 1980:6). This boast acquired new meaning as a result of the demonstrations in Angola and Ethiopia that the Soviet Union and its allies could support and direct successful, large-scale military operations in countries far from Soviet borders.* Never again would strategic inferiority or a lack of power projection capabilities force Soviet leaders to accept embarrassing defeats such as occurred in the early 1960s, when Nikita Khrushchev was unable to support Patrice Lumumba and his followers in Congo/Kinshasa (Zaire).

Second, the self-proclaimed Marxist-Leninist character of the regimes in Angola, Ethiopia, and Mozambique sparked a debate in both the West and East over the prospects for and significance of scientific socialism in Africa.† Carl Rosberg and Thomas Callaghy argued that socialism in sub-Saharan Africa had entered "a new

---

*On the extent and significance of improvements in Soviet power projection capabilities, see Porter (1984:36-59), and Stefansky (1985).

†Sixteen years after Marien Ngouabi declared the Congo to be a "People's Republic" guided by Marxism-Leninism, there is still no agreement among scholars over what to call such regimes. Some have adopted the term "Afrocommunist," which was first coined by David and Marina Ottaway in 1981 (see Ottaway and Ottaway 1981). Others, following Crawford Young, use the term "Afro-Marxist" (see Young 1982). Another group rejects both of these labels, arguing that it is the "Leninist" organizational character of these regimes rather than their commitment to a Marxist or Communist project that distinguishes them from other Third World regimes (for example, see Valenta and Valenta 1984). There is yet another group of analysts who reject almost entirely the claim that regimes such as those in Angola, Ethiopia, and Mozambique — much less those in the Congo and Benin — can usefully be called Communist, Marxist, or Leninist (for example, see Jowitt 1979). There is unquestionably a fundamental difference between the "radical" socialism of Angola, Ethiopia, and Mozambique and the more "reformist" socialism of states such as Senegal and Zambia. However, whether Angola, Ethiopia, Mozambique, or any other "radical socialist" regime in Africa can be usefully called "Communist," "Marxist," or "Leninist" is uncertain. In this volume, therefore, we have chosen to use the more open-ended label, "radical socialist." (On the general problem of determining whether regimes are Communist, see Kautsky 1973, Harding 1981, and White 1983).

phase," distinguished by the decisions of governments such as those in Angola, Ethiopia, and Mozambique to opt for scientific socialism and attempt to create effective Marxist-Leninist vanguard parties (1979:1-11). Similarly, Ottaway and Ottaway referred to the mid-1970s as "an historic turning point in the tortuous development of socialism inside Africa" (1981:7). This judgment was echoed by a diverse array of other Western analysts.* There was, however, no agreement concerning the causes and implications of these two changes.

Western analysts divided into two major groups: (1) Conservative globalists, who viewed the Soviet interventions and the emergence of a new group of radical socialist states in Africa with considerable alarm, seeing these developments as part of a growing global threat to Western interests in the Third World; and (2) Skeptical regionalists, who explained Soviet intervention in situational rather than predispositional terms and discounted the "socialist" pretensions of the regimes in Angola, Ethiopia, and Mozambique.† A third group also emerged—"enthusiasts," who were sympathetic with the new re-

---

*For example, see Young (1982:22-96) and Radu (1982). For a review of this literature, see Clough (1984).

†Since the late 1970s many scholars have used the terms "regionalist" and "globalist" to characterize differing U.S. policy perspectives on Africa. For example, Donald Rothchild and John Ravenhill wrote as follows: "Regionalists perceive African problems with a sympathetic eye, placing emphasis on the uniqueness of the African environment and attempting to accommodate the aspirations of African peoples. Globalists, on the other hand, tend to perceive African issues from the perspective of an all-encompassing East-West conflict in which there can be no neutral parties" (1983). This dichotomy is false and misleading. It implies that the only issue is whether policymakers and analysts focus on the regional dimension of African problems or the global dimension. In practice, the conflict is not just between regionalists and globalists but among a more diverse array of protagonists with varying views of regional realities and global considerations. Both regionalists and globalists come in different varieties. For example, there are "liberal" regionalists (e.g., Andrew Young) and "conservative" regionalists (e.g., Chester Crocker), and there are "ideological" globalists (e.g., Jeane Kirkpatrick) and "cynical" globalists (e.g., Richard Pipes). Reducing the policy debate to a regionalist/globalist debate begs too many questions. It fails to recognize that (1) U.S. policy toward Africa will always be based in part on global considerations, and that (2) There are legitimate grounds for disagreement concerning the nature of regional realities. In this study we have sought to capture the nuances of the policy debate by qualifying our usage of the terms regionalist and globalist. "Conservative globalist," as used in this chapter, designates someone who is primarily concerned with the impact of

gimes' plans to build socialism but had little impact on the Western policy debate (for example, see Saul 1985, Isaacman and Isaacman 1983a, and Wolfers and Bergerol 1983). Below we outline the major viewpoints of the two major groups.

The Conservative Globalist View. Conservative globalists perceived the rise of radical socialism in Africa in terms of a continuing Soviet drive to undermine Western influence and establish Marxist-Leninist beachheads in the Third World. Their argument begins from strongly held assumptions about Soviet predispositions and proceeds to criticism of Western leaders for lack of resolve. The Soviet Union is portrayed as an internally decaying, ideologically driven, and hence inherently expansionist global power. Such a power cannot be accommodated diplomatically or otherwise; it can only be blocked militarily.* Soviet "gains" in Africa and elsewhere are in this view primarily the result of failures of the United States to stand up to Soviet challenges. For example, conservative globalists attribute the MPLA's victory in Angola to the refusal of a "neoisolationist" U.S. Congress, immobilized by exaggerated fears of "another Vietnam," to support the Ford administration's efforts to counter Soviet and Cuban intervention (Revel 1985:114; see also Kiracofe 1982 and Vanneman and James 1976).

Success in Angola (following this argument) caused the Soviet Union to embark on even bolder adventures elsewhere—e.g., Ethiopia and Afghanistan. Developments in Angola, Ethiopia, and Mozambique, along with those in Nicaragua, Afghanistan, and Kampuchea, according to one conservative globalist, Alex Alexiev,

---

developments in Africa on the global balance of power and believes that the use of force, actual or threatened, is the major determinant of regional outcomes. A "skeptical regionalist" is someone whose perception of developments in Africa is strongly conditioned by a belief in the largely intractable nature of African realities *and* the limited ability of either superpower to influence regional actors. On the fundamental sources of differing Western assessments of the Soviet threat in Africa, see Jordan (1985). For a very useful attempt to categorize U.S. policy prescriptions for Africa, see Kitchen (1979).

*Among the most influential recent general statements of the conservative globalist position are Luttwak (1983), Revel (1985), and Pipes (1984). The classic official statement of conservative globalism is NSC 68, a memo prepared for President Harry Truman in 1950; see Etzold and Gaddis (1978:385-442). Among the major conservative globalist writings on Africa are Rothenberg (1980), Henriksen, ed. (1981), Pearson, ed. (1977), Thompson (1980), and Hahn and Cottrell (1977).

formed part of "a new Soviet offensive against the West in the Third World" (1982:2). Unless halted by decisive Western—i.e., American— actions, this offensive would continue to build momentum, the conservative globalists predicted. Frances Fukuyama puts it as follows:

> The problem for the West is not simply that communist gains in these apparently remote countries threaten specific Western interests, but that they have the potential to become cumulative and self-reinforcing. The Soviets are in the process of constructing what amounts to a multinational military infrastructure which can be used as a base of operations for further expansion" (1979:57).

Conservative globalists are sharply critical of radical socialist states in Africa—and elsewhere. In their view, the ideological orientation of the new Marxist-Leninist regimes in the Third World must be taken seriously because it "has led to a striking consistency in both their political structure and behavior, which clearly sets them apart as a group and differentiates them from the non-communist Soviet client regimes of earlier decades" (Fukuyama 1984:3). Marxism-Leninism provides "a ready blueprint for reordering society toward egalitarianism and for attaining power against opposition" (Henriksen 1981:115-16). The political/organizational ("totalitarian") character of Afrocommunism is a particular concern of many conservative globalists. Henriksen writes the following:

> In their zeal, the new Afrocommunist governments seek to transplant the orthodox features of communist states, such as the party structure, from local cells to central committees, a system of party congresses, neighborhood vigilance groups, mass organizations, and the secret police (1981:115-16).

Increasing resistance and intensifying repression are inevitable, conservative globalists argue, because Marxism-Leninism is an ideology alien to Africa that has been imposed on hapless populations by narrowly based urban elites aided and abetted by the Soviet Union and its "surrogates," especially Cuba and East Germany. In each of the new Marxist-Leninist regimes in the Third World, Jeane Kirkpatrick argues,

> the revolutionary government has sought to transform traditional ways of life ... to fit socialist goals and blueprints. This further enhances the sense that aliens' rule is seeking to wipe out indigenous cultures. In each, economic disorganization, stagnation, and

scarcity have followed on the heels of installation of a communist government; so has military mobilization of the country. In each, the population of political prisoners has greatly increased as has the flow of refugees fleeing the new order. In each, the government itself has come to power by force, and maintains itself in power by force (1985:92).

What worries conservative globalists most is the relation between radical socialist regimes and the Soviet Union. According to Fukuyama (1984:4), the new Marxist-Leninist Third World states have (1) Followed a course of "socialist internationalism" involving close alignment with the Soviet Union and its allies and strong support for fellow Marxist-Leninist regimes and progressive national liberation movements, and (2) Shown a strong inclination to cooperate with the armed forces of the USSR.

If Afrocommunism is not "contained" (or, as some would prefer, "rolled back"), conservative globalists argue it will eventually threaten Western economic interests—particularly access to minerals—endanger the security of shipping lanes, and destabilize countries friendly to the West like Sudan, Zaire, and South Africa (see Hanks 1983).

The Skeptical Regionalist View. In the view of skeptical regionalists Soviet successes in Africa grew out of opportunities created by local situations. The Soviet Union is portrayed as a powerful but insecure state seeking to establish its credentials as a superpower on par with the United States.* The changes in the strategic balance and the growth of Soviet power projection capabilities which occurred in the decade prior to 1975 are regarded as necessary but not sufficient causes of Soviet intervention. Instead skeptical regionalists focus on the dynamics of individual conflicts and local actors. For example, Colin Legum argued that "external intervention in Africa is made possible, and usually produced, by Africans themselves. Africans are not . . . simply passive victims of major powers; they themselves now constitute the agents who introduce foreign powers into the continent's conflicts" (1980:14).†

---

*For assessments of Soviet foreign policy that are generally consistent with the skeptical regionalist position, see Garthoff (1985), Shulman (1973), and Legvold (1977 and 1979).

†For other examples of the skeptical regionalist perspective, see Marcum (1985), Kitchen (1983), Nation and Kauppi, eds. (1984), Albright (1983), Bienen (1982), Nolutshungu (1982), and Singleton (1980).

Typical of the skeptical regionalist interpretation of the Angolan civil war was that of Cyrus Vance:

[Secretary Henry Kissinger's] preoccupation with the problem of managing the increasingly complex and multifaceted equilibrium among the United States, the Soviet Union, the PRC, western Europe, and Japan distorted his initial view of the problems of Third World conflict and change. This caused him to misjudge the Angola crisis of 1975, which he interpreted almost entirely in terms of the East-West rivalry. His failure to focus on the local causes of the Angolan civil war, the profound nationalism of the Angolan forces of whatever ideological coloration, his insistence on viewing the struggle ... as a battle in the larger East-West geopolitical competition, led him to take actions and positions that reduced our ability to maneuver. In the end, the strongest nationalist faction was left with no alternative but dependence on Soviet, and eventually Cuban, assistance for survival (1983:24; see also Bender 1981 and Marcum 1978).

With regard to Ethiopia, skeptical regionalists argue as follows: Soviet leaders were once again responding to an urgent plea for assistance, only in this instance their ability to legitimate their intervention by invoking the right of sovereign states to call on outside powers for defensive assistance was even stronger than in the Angolan case. Had it not been for the Somali invasion, the Soviet and Cuban operation would not have occurred (see Garthoff 1985:630-52, Brind 1983-84, and Vance 1983:72-75, 85-88). In both cases, regionalists tend to downplay the importance of Western inaction as a cause of Soviet and Cuban intervention. In addition, some regionalists argue that U.S. actions were partially responsible for setting in motion the events that led to the Soviet interventions. A January 1975 decision by the Ford administration to provide limited covert aid to the FNLA may have inadvertently encouraged Roberto and his supporters to believe they could count on American support for their attempt to eliminate the MPLA by military means (Marcum 1978:258). Similarly, vague promises of "defensive" military assistance made by officials in the Carter administration may have contributed to the Somali decision to invade Ethiopia (Garthoff 1985:633-37).

Skeptical regionalists reject the conservative globalist view that the outcomes in Angola and Ethiopia led to substantial Soviet gains elsewhere on the continent. In fact, Seth Singleton has argued that the Soviets began to lose rather than gain influence in 1977-78 (1980:360 and 1982:188, 234). Sam Nolutshungu contends that "Despite Angola, Ethiopia and Mozambique, no fundamental change has occurred in the nature of Soviet-American relations" (1982:414). Both of these assessments rest on the argument that after the mid-1970s situational factors became increasingly less conducive to successful Soviet intervention.

Soviet influence, according to the regionalist argument, has remained strong only in those countries where incumbent regimes have faced continuing threats to their security. "Soviet power," argues Henry Bienen, "is most secure in a country where the regime is highly insecure" (1982:171). Internal and regional threats, rather than ideological affinity, are regarded as the main impetus behind the decisions of Angola, Ethiopia, and Mozambique to sign treaties of friendship and cooperation with the Soviet Union. For example, in 1977, facing possible security threats from Rhodesia and South Africa, FRELIMO decided that "the Soviet Union rather than China had the military logistical capacity required of a strategic ally" (Legum 1984:21).

Skeptical regionalists are generally less worried than conservative globalists about the threat to Western interests posed by the decision of Third World regimes to declare themselves Marxist-Leninist. They believe that the rhetoric of radical socialists is taken too seriously by both critics and supporters of such regimes. The adoption of the "scientific socialist" designation should be viewed as an attempt to gain status, domestically and internationally, and extract resources and secure support from the Eastern bloc.* Skeptical regionalists believe that nationalism and regime survival, not Marxism-Leninism, determine the foreign policies of radical socialist states (for example, see Legum 1980 and Shoemaker and Spanier 1984).

An increasingly dominant strand in the skeptical regionalist argument is the contention that the options open to African leaders, especially in the economic realm, are so limited that it is misleading to pay too much attention to ideological declarations. For example, Rosberg and Callaghy have written the following:

> The economies of African socialist states remain dependent on and integrated into the world capitalist economy. . . . Economic autarky is not a viable option. Heavily dependent on commodity trade, they are also dependent on outside sources for capital

---

*The best statement of this argument is Jowitt (1979).

accumulation, technical assistance, and investment plans. The relations between socialist states and multinational corporations appear to be little different from those in non-socialist states. Despite the ideological ties and orientation of scientific socialist African states with external socialist powers, no dramatic economic alternatives have become available (1979:6; see also Price 1978:14-29 and Feinberg 1983:82-140).

While concerned about political repression and economic dislocations in radical socialist states, skeptical regionalists disagree with the harsh criticisms of these regimes expressed by Kirkpatrick and other conservatives on three grounds. First, they argue that such criticisms overstate the differences between conditions in Angola, Ethiopia, and Mozambique, on the one hand, and conditions in many nonsocialist African states like Zaire and Liberia, on the other hand. Second, they point out that the situations in Angola and Mozambique are in part the result of years of Portuguese neglect and the massive exodus of Portuguese settlers at independence, an exodus that was only in part due to the actions of the MPLA and FRELIMO (for example, see Bender 1978:7-8). Finally, they argue that conditions in all three of these countries have been exacerbated by drought and external intervention. They point out that political and economic conditions in radical socialist states such as the Congo compare favorably with those in most nonsocialist African states, thus challenging the view that radical socialism per se is the problem in Angola, Ethiopia, and Mozambique.*

Which of these assessments, the conservative globalist or the skeptical regionalist, has proven more accurate? One of the main objectives of this volume is to answer this question. Sufficient time has now passed since the Angolan civil war of 1975 to allow a judgment on the basis of historical evidence rather than mere speculation. In their essays on Angola, Ethiopia, and Mozambique, John Marcum, Paul Henze, and Martin Lowenkopf examine developments in each of these critical countries from the mid-1970s through 1985. In the concluding essay Michael Clough examines the Soviet record in Africa since 1975 in broader terms and assesses the likely effects of alternative U.S. policies toward radical socialist states in Africa.

---

*The most thoughtful attempt to compare the performance of different types of African regimes is Young (1982).

BIPOLAR DEPENDENCY: THE PEOPLE'S REPUBLIC OF ANGOLA

John Marcum

Entering its second decade of independence, insurgency-torn Angola confronts the contradictions of a concurrent dependency on the military power of the Soviet Union and Cuba and the economic and technological power of the United States and Western Europe. This double dependency pulls Angola simultaneously in opposite directions.

The social origins and historical experience of the governing Movimento Popular de Libertação de Angola (MPLA) pointed to a post-independence ideological and political association with Soviet-linked Communist states. Economic needs and possibilities, however, provided a rationale for preserving and ultimately expanding ties to Western markets, capital, and technology. Over time the bipolar pull between ideological, political, and security commitments on the one hand and commercial and technological links on the other has tried Angolan government unity and divided Angolan society.

Is it possible in a sustained manner to juxtapose a political security and defense system dependent on Soviet, Cuban, and East German personnel and materiel with a petroleum-based economic system dependent on Western corporate and banking institutions? Or is such segmented dependency inherently unstable? Prevailing leadership in the avowedly Marxist-Leninist MPLA assumes that it is possible to seal off Angolan political institutions from a possibly subversive intrusion of Western values and practices disseminated through economic relations. Conflict between incompatible social values and competing external linkages, however, must inevitably spill over into the realms of education, press, cultural life, and social organization. Bipolar dependency thus seems likely to foster deep-seated instability until it is either superseded by an overall ascendency on the part of one of the contending tendencies or displaced by the successful emergence of a cohesive Angolan government possessed of the will, skill, and guile with which to diversify and manage external dependency to its own advantage.

In assessing the dynamics and possible outcome of Angola's bipolar dependency, it is important to consider how and why a fledgling African state has found itself in such circumstances. The following analysis looks at the origins and nature of Angola's socialist option, the extent and character of its external dependency, and the forces likely to determine its future ideological, economic, and strategic orientation.

ORIGINS OF ANGOLA'S SOCIALIST OPTION

Of all the nationalist movements that led sub-Saharan colonies into independence after World War II, the MPLA can make the strongest claim to significant (but not wholly) Marxist roots. A Product of that sector of Angolan society most fully integrated into the Portuguese-dominated colonial economy, the MPLA included among its initial constituents a number of small, class-conscious urban groups founded or influenced by Portuguese and Brazilian Marxists—teachers, civil servants, commercial employees. Members of these groups drew upon their reading and interpretation of Marxist-Leninist literature as they molded organizational structure and strategies.

Under the personalized autocracy of António Salazar (1933-68), Portuguese authorities severely repressed cultural as well as political expression in their African colonies. Given the limitations of Portugal's own economic and educational backwardness, its administrators felt obliged to resort to crude coercion and mercantilism to hold on to a little-developed but exploitable empire. Refusing to emulate timely British, French, and Belgian concessions to emergent sub-Saharan nationalism for fear of losing their privileged economic position, they rejected American and other criticism of their rigid colonial policies. They dismissed external criticism as motivated by a desire to open the door to competing economic ambitions. A predictable consequence of their rigidity was the radicalization of frustrated, disaffected Africans, leading to the outbreak of armed insurgency in Angola (1961), Guinea-Bissau (1963), and Mozambique (1964).

Despite police repression, travel restrictions, and the inherent constraints of illiteracy (90 percent) and poverty in Angola, word of political change outside and increasing consciousness of social injustice inside spurred clandestine political activity. This activity was most intensive in Luanda, the core of a relatively modernized "central society" incorporated within the colonial political economy.* There, according to contemporary MPLA and Soviet accounts, young Angolans exposed to Marxist thought responded to increasing political coercion by forming political groups of a "revolutionary character" (Andrade 1960: 34). One enthusiastic but far-removed Soviet observer wrote of a Marxist underground that during 1955-56 created "hundreds of mobile libraries" and clandestine schools in "the African quarters of Luanda" (Sidenko 1961).

In December 1956 the MPLA emerged as an umbrella movement assembling disparate nationalist groups in Luanda and lesser urban centers within a single, coherent organizational and action framework. Among its constituent elements was a diminutive Partido Comunista de Angola (PCA) that had been formed a year earlier. Portuguese Communists, like their French counterparts, had been slow to embrace the cause of African nationalism, and formation of the PCA seems to have represented an independent effort by local Marxists to assert a leading role in the mobilization of a broad-based anticolonial movement.† Though prominently noted in Soviet publications of the early 1960s,** the PCA would subsequently be described by Soviet field researchers as having been a group of just over a dozen persons (interviews, Moscow, June-July 1984).††

---

*As distinguished from the majoritarian "tributary societies" of traditional peasants and herders in which nationalism was slower to develop and assumed a more ethnocentric or sectional focus. See Heimer (1979: 12-16).

†In the words of one-time MPLA representative (early 1970s) in Scandinavia, António Alberto Neto, the PCA was formed after the Portuguese Communist Party had failed to follow appropriate "proletarian internationalism" with respect to Portugal's colonies. A year after the PCA's formation, its leaders helped to form the MPLA, a "broad front" within which they assumed leadership roles "at the head" of the MPLA's internal and external organization (A. A. Neto 1967: 35-36).

**According to the Soviet handbook *Africa Today* (1962), the MPLA was founded "on the initiative of the Communist Party" and an "allied" Partido da Luta dos Africanos de Angola (translated in *Mizan Newsletter* [London] 4, 5 [April 1962]). See also Sidenko (1960) and *International Affairs* (Moscow) 7, 3 (March 1961).

††No comparable political group emerged in Mozambique, where white settlement was half that of Angola and the colonial educational and economic system was even more rudimentary.

Unlike African nationalist movements that began with little more than an opportunistic, tactical link to European Communists (Ivory Coast) or an essentially rhetorical nod to socialism (Ghana), the MPLA included among its principal founders men with a genuinely sophisticated grasp of Marxist-Leninist thought—persons such as Lúcio Lara, Mário de Andrade, and Viriato da Cruz.* Though more pragmatic and accommodating in his political style, Agostinho Neto, the MPLA's president from 1962 until his death in 1979, was also deeply influenced by an exposure to left-wing, anti-Salazar thought and politics as a medical student in Portugal.† After he escaped Portugal and assumed the presidency of the MPLA, Neto undertook a bridge-building tour of Western Europe and the United States. But his tour failed to generate significant Western support. Neto ascribed this failure to the forces of "western imperialism" and came to rely heavily on small-scale but sustained material and diplomatic assistance from the Soviet Union and allied "socialist countries."

American officials would later estimate that up to April 1974, when a military coup overthrew the Lisbon government, the value of Soviet arms and other material support for the MPLA totaled approximately $63 million (interview with officials, Department of State, Washington, D.C., 1 December 1975). Soviet political support ranged from international conferences on Portuguese colonialism** to military and technical training for hundreds of MPLA militants to MPLA use of Soviet embassy communications facilities. In a candid acknowledgment of Soviet aims, *Pravda*'s T. Kolesnichenko wrote in 1965 that by assisting the MPLA, socialist states were "playing an important part in spreading the ideas of socialism and revolutionary anticolonial ideology" (*Pravda*, 22 April 1965).

From the MPLA's vantage point, its socialist option was determined as much by Western hostility as by Soviet blandishments.

---

*Evidence of the sophistication can be seen in the following: (1) Lara (1963); Slovo interview with Lara (1978); (2) Andrade (1966); Andrade and Ollivier (1971); and (3) da Cruz (1964 and 1962).

†Neto was arrested in Portugal in 1952 because of his participation on the central committee of an anti-Salazar youth group, the Movimento de Unidade Democrática-Juvenil. He was an off- and on-again political prisoner throughout the next decade.

**For example, the International Conference of Support to the Peoples of the Portuguese Colonies, Rome, 27-29 June 1970, organized by the World Peace Council in support of the MPLA and allied nationalists of Mozambique and Guinea-Bissau.

A Soviet-initiated blockade of West Berlin in 1961 prompted an airlift from the United States that dramatized the value of Azores logistical bases to Western defense. Rather than risk access to these bases, American officials curbed criticism of Portugal's colonial policies, and the United States played the role of a relatively passive NATO ally (no counterinsurgency assistance but also little pressure for colonial reform) for the duration of Portugal's African rule.

What little sympathy or support the American government extended to Angolan nationalists went to the MPLA's competitors. Between 1962 and 1969 Washington reportedly invested covert assistance (measured in thousands not millions of dollars) in the insurgent Frente Nacional de Libertação de Angola (FNLA), a movement led by a Bakongo emigre (i.e., from northern Angola) and declared anti-Communist, Holden Roberto.* Though it probably overestimated American commitment and assistance to Roberto, the MPLA understandably assumed that the pro-FNLA stance of the strongly U.S.-backed government of Zaire's President Mobutu Sésé Séko also reflected American policy.† Mobutu persistently crushed all efforts by MPLA insurgents to establish logistical bases in Zaire such as those enjoyed by the FNLA.

By the mid-1960s American foreign policymakers concluded that early estimates of the effectiveness and potential of the Angolan insurgency had been inflated. Portuguese resolve and Angolan frailties, they decided, were such that the Angolans could not win (see el-Khawas and Cohen, eds. 1976). Convincing themselves that with time gradual reform would blunt the thrust of revolutionary action, complacent American officials failed to perceive the signs of Portuguese war fatigue (inflation, emigration, military desertions, sabotage) that had been induced by escalating insurgency in Guinea-Bissau and Mozambique and was paving the way for the military coup of 1974.

Following the Lisbon coup, U.S.-linked Zaire increased its assistance to the FNLA. According to Lara, as early as December

---

*In 1969 the Nixon administration reduced this already modest assistance to Roberto to a retainer fee of just a few thousand dollars a year (*New York Times*, 25 September and 19 December 1975).

†In mid-1963, when the MPLA perceived the United States as particularly hostile, State Department Circular 92 (16 July 1963) stated that the U.S. government should "seek to gain the confidence of both" the FNLA and MPLA and advised against becoming "embroiled" in efforts to choose between them or to press them into a common front.

1974 Zairean troops began crossing the border into northern Angola.* Zaire also helped to orchestrate attempts to replace Neto and his Luanda-centered MPLA organization as an externally recognized Angolan contender for political power with a dissident MPLA faction led by Daniel Chipenda and headquartered at the time in Kinshasa.†

As Portuguese authority subsequently waned and ultimately vanished during 1974-75, the FNLA managed to deploy a partly Chinese-trained army throughout the northern (Bakongo) part of the country. A third contender, the black nationalist and regionally based União para a Independencia Total de Angola (UNITA), founded in 1966 by a young Ovimbundu leader, Jonas Savimbi, moved to establish a political hold on cities and towns of the populous (Ovimbundu) central highlands.

Having suffered military reverses and fallen victim to political factionalism, the MPLA was in a particularly vulnerable condition at the time of the 1974 Lisbon coup. Under Neto's leadership it had to scramble to reorganize and survive. In so doing, it enjoyed one significant advantage: its principal stronghold was the political, commercial, and communications center of the country, Luanda, and its (ethnic Mbundu) hinterland.

Seasoned external ties and affinities now asserted themselves. The United States foresook diplomatic efforts either to secure an intra-Angolan tripartite accommodation with free elections or to reach an understanding with the Soviet Union designed to avoid a winner-take-all contest for power. Washington began channeling financial support to the FNLA through Zaire. The Soviets resumed military assistance to the MPLA which they had cut in 1972-73, when the MPLA had fallen into a state of disarray. Even more important, Cuba, since the mid-1960s the MPLA's most unflagging, ideologically committed provider of military and technical

---

*Portuguese authorities had little respect for Zaire's ill-disciplined military, concluded that they could push Zairean troops out and secure the northern border at will, and consequently failed to act on MPLA appeals for their prompt expulsion (interviews with Portuguese observers, Lisbon, May 1985).

†Mobutu successfully championed Chipenda's cause in mid-September 1974 discussions with Portuguese provisional President António de Spínola in the Cape Verde Islands. But Spínola was forced out of office before he could engineer recognition of the Chipenda faction as *the* MPLA.

training, responded to appeals for stepped-up support.* For its part, UNITA, which had never had a large armed force and which adopted a post-coup political strategy designed to win elections promised by Portugal, became desperate by mid-1975. It faced possible military annihilation and looked frantically for outside assistance. *Faut de mieux* it turned fatefully to South Africa to help it build an army of its own. South Africa, eager to reverse the advance of a perceived Soviet and Cuban "onslaught," responded dramatically.

If the exact sequence of external intervention remains arguable, its genesis and consequences seem clear-cut. During the 1960s and early 1970s insurgency in Portuguese Africa had offered the Soviets and Cubans promising conditions for revolutionary proselytizing— conditions that had not heretofore been available to them in sub-Saharan Africa. In 1975 the flight of resident Portuguese from Angola prior to independence and the related prospects for a military as distinct from electoral contest for political power offered the Soviets and Cubans an opportunity to play their "revolutionary" trump card—direct military intervention. However, as Soviet arms and Cuban troops poured in by sea and air from the north, South African forces swept up from the south—some said with American encouragement (*New York Times*, 6 February 1976; *Sunday Telegraph* [London], 7 February 1977). But for an opportunistic and massive Soviet/Cuban airlift, the MPLA would have been wiped out by the South Africans. Instead, as foreign journalists uncovered evidence of a secretive intervention by forces from apartheid South Africa, potentially strong opposition to Soviet and Cuban intervention by African states dissipated.

With a massive delivery of men and materiel, Soviet air and sea power demonstrated a stunning new global outreach. The United States flinched in the face of the possible cost of underwriting a war by dubious proxies. The poorly led FNLA collapsed. South Africa withdrew. UNITA pulled back into the forest and bush of the lightly populated southeast. The MPLA, saved by its long-time external benefactors, proclaimed the People's Republic of Angola (PRA) on 11 November 1975, and turned to the task of constructing the socialist society that some of its founders had been advocating for two decades.

*For a Soviet description of Cuba's role as both independent (not Soviet-instigated) and principled, see Kokorev (1979); for a balanced American analysis that confirms independent Cuban initiative within a context of enabling Soviet support, see LeoGrande (1980).

ANGOLAN SOCIALISM: RHETORIC OR REALITY?

The departure of all but perhaps 10 percent of the 350,000 Portuguese who had been running the country cleared (and nearly destroyed) the economic deck. Taking their commercial vehicles and anything else they could move to Portugal with them, Portuguese *retornados* left Angola bereft of managerial and technical skills. Their departure also removed any propertied opposition to a radical restructuring of the economy.

Before it could build a new socialist system, the MPLA had to secure its political authority. It had to do so under conditions of economic extremity. The physical and human devastation of the 1975 civil war had coupled with the massive Portuguese exodus to bring transportation, commerce, and production to a standstill.

During the months following the Lisbon coup, the veteran leadership of the MPLA, whose organization had finally been legalized by the Portuguese, had brought new cadres of educated blacks and *mestiços* into its organization. Simultaneously, it had organized among uprooted, ex-peasant slum dwellers who had migrated into towns during the war-induced economic growth of the 1960s and early 1970s. Cleavage between these social strata became a source of division within the MPLA that could be exploited by radical elements ambitious for political power. Led by Nito Alves, organizer of "power to the people" political action groups in Luanda, MPLA *"fraccionistas"* resorted to racial demagoguery in manipulating discontent over food shortages. They alleged fumbling management on the part of an ideologically lax MPLA administration whose ranks accorded an undue prominence to a white and mestiço elite.

Politically contained by senior MPLA leadership, frustrated Nitista radicals mounted a bloody but unsuccessful coup in May 1977. The coup's failure left the government in place but further weakened. Significantly, the fact that Alves, an advocate of closer ties to the Soviet Union, had had frequent contact with the Soviet and Cuban embassies raised questions about the reliability of the MPLA's external mentors.*

---

*According to informed accounts, neither the Soviet nor the Cuban embassy provided a forewarning of Alves's intentions to mount a coup, and Luanda exacted the recall of both the Soviet and Cuban ambassadors. For an official MPLA account of the coup which acknowledges that Alves's fraccionistas influenced diplomats from "friendly countries," see MPLA (1977).

In spite of being further weakened, the MPLA proceeded with previously set plans to hold its first congress in 1977. Already in 1975 the PRA constitution had asserted the primacy of the MPLA as a "broad front" of "anti-imperialist" forces mandated to lead the country toward a society free from "exploitation of man by man" (PRA, Ministry of Information 1976). In October 1976 the MPLA Central Committee determined that a path-setting congress should be held in 1977, at which time the MPLA would be converted into a "party guided by Marxism-Leninism, the ideology of the proletariat" (MPLA 1976).

According to Lara, haste and fervor in the push to create a Marxist-Leninist party were attributable in large measure to pressure from embittered MPLA militants who wanted to retaliate against the "anti-Communist" intervention of South Africa, Zaire, and the United States (interview, Luanda, October 1984; see also Brittain 1984). Relatively few members of the MPLA had been introduced even to such basic Marxist concepts as dialectical materialism. Yet the adherence of thousands of MPLA followers to the pursuit of "scientific socialism" was declared an accomplished fact on the basis of popular "trust" in the MPLA and in the "guidance of Comrade President Agostinho Neto" (MPLA 1977). Party membership was accordingly left accessible to the unindoctrinated, and membership in mass organizations for labor, women, youth, etc. was not to require even nominal adherence to Marxist-Leninist ideology—at least not in the near term.

On 10 December 1977, its twenty-first birthday, the MPLA became a party "guided by the scientific ideology of the proletariat, Marxism-Leninism"—the MPLA-Partido do Trabalho/MPLA-PT (MPLA 1977). To be built upon a base of cells with three to thirty members, the MPLA-PT assumed a standard Communist party structure topped by a political bureau elected by a central committee chosen by a party congress, elected, in turn, by local party organs. Underscoring a formal commitment to Marxist-Leninist orthodoxy, the new "vanguard" party rejected the concepts of "African socialism" and Pan-Africanism as regressive and parochial and pledged to follow a proper "internationalist" path to true "scientific socialism."

MPLA party leaders gave urgent priority to political education and the revival of agriculture, the livelihood of some 85 percent of the population. But such efforts ran into a wall of grim realities. The agricultural marketing system had evaporated with the departure of Portuguese traders. Local cadres, even when reinforced by Cubans and other foreigners, were insufficient to revive it, and an ideological rejection of market incentives discouraged voluntaristic solutions. The dislocations of war, disorganization of government services, and peasant hostility to imposed collectivization defied utopian plans. Previously a food exporter, Angola became (and remains) an importer of over 80 percent of its commercial food supplies.

The survival and then dramatic growth of UNITA caught the MPLA in a vicious circle. UNITA's resilient insurgents were able to shut down the Benguela railroad, demolish towns over a great swath of the southeast, and raid, ambush, and sabotage within the agricultural country of the central highlands of UNITA's home political bailiwick. The MPLA's inability to deliver goods and services to regions of the interior contributed to political dissidence. UNITA guerrillas exploited this dissidence in their campaigns to disrupt transportation, promote insecurity, and uproot thousands of peasants. These actions in turn undercut government efforts to revive the food production and distribution necessary to build popular support and reduce political dissidence.

MPLA authorities later acknowledged that early in their rule overly zealous, by-the-book centralization had dulled sensitivity to rural needs and slowed the implantation of the party outside of "detribalized" urban centers. With disarming candor, they accepted that urban socialists in a hurry to collectivize and mechanize had initially undervalued peasant views. Inexperienced administrators were responsible for "tremendous errors in agriculture—bad decisions, improvisations and waste" (Brittain 1984).

Prolonged agricultural disaster ultimately induced open and widespread party debate over agricultural policy and greater flexibility in the government's approach—for example, a turn to smaller producer cooperatives. Increased technical help along with financial incentives became available to small producers of coffee, cotton, and maize. The government launched efforts to rebuild the defunct retail trading system. MPLA Organizing Secretary and Marxist theoretician Lara became involved in intense but inconclusive efforts to resurrect and reorganize coffee production, which fell from 5.2 million sacks in 1974 to 283,000 sacks in 1984. Lara even expressed a new appreciation for prescriptive, nonideological pragmatism, such as that of French agronomist René Dumont, author of *L'Afrique noire est mal partie,* and warned against the stifling effects of excessive party bureaucracy (Brittain 1984 and interview, Luanda, November 1985).

While the agricultural core of Angola's traditional economy floundered, the country was kept afloat by the oil produced by and sold to Western private enterprise. Despite the mayhem of civil war and subsequent American government refusal to recognize the PRA, Gulf Oil Corporation continued the production of Cabindan oil that it had begun under the Portuguese. By the time of independence, Angolan oil revenue had reached approximately $400 million a year. The MPLA government renegotiated the Gulf contract, acquiring a 51 percent interest in Cabinda Gulf for its state oil company, Sonangol. The contract established a precedent for other joint undertakings that would draw upon Western technology and capital. One result was a systematic expansion of petroleum exploration and production that pushed up Angolan oil revenue, which reached $2 billion in 1984. The United States imported 53 percent of the 1984 production. American private banks provided some $200 million in short- and long-term financing for Sonangol operations. The U.S. government's Export-Import Bank lent even more. Prospects for a steady expansion of Angolan oil (and natural gas) production and sales to the United States, Western Europe, and Brazil appeared excellent.

American banks and corporations found the Angolan government to be an uncommonly honest, if tough, bargainer. Cordial commercial relations developed despite the absence of diplomatic relations. Arthur D. Little, Inc. contracted to act as a financial consultant to the government and to run training courses for its technocrats. Western Europeans expanded their involvement in Angola. Elf and Total (France) operate in the northern coast oil fields; Austro-Mineral (Austria) has undertaken to revive iron ore production at Kassinga; Spanish fishing interests have helped to rebuild the southern fishing industry in exchange for shrimping rights. A Brazilian company, Norberto Oderbracht, has contracted to build a $500 million hydroelectric dam at Kapande on the Cuanza River, and two-way Angolan-Brazilian trade reached $230 million in 1984.

The contribution of some five thousand Cuban teachers, doctors, engineers, and technicians and the participation of the Soviets in such development projects as the Kapande dam aside, the role of Communist states in Angola (as elsewhere in Africa) has been primarily military. They have not provided a level of economic assistance that might permit Angola to break out of its economic distress. They have left Angolans dependent on a Western-oriented oil economy.

In the view of doctrinaire leftist critics, the PRA has bowed to short-run pressures and accorded "foreign monopoly capital" a role incompatible with Marxist-Leninist principles. In the process, the ruling MPLA has thus demonstrated itself to be a "petty bourgeois intellectual" organization whose practice is irreconcilable with its theory. Pragmatism has prevailed over ideology (Makidi-Ku-Ntima 1983).

Impressed by the open, businesslike manner with which Angolan officials have approached relations with them, some American corporate observers have also tended to see Angolan socialism as more rhetorical than real. Pointing to such indicators as the PRA's entry into the Lomé Treaty association with the European Community, they have concluded that only Angola's dependence on the Soviet Union and Cuba for defense and security prevents it from forsaking an increasingly nominal commitment to Marxism-Leninism in favor of demonstrably more rewarding, Western-oriented economic pragmatism.

SECURITY AND DEFENSE: THE OVERRIDING DEPENDENCY?

Soviet publications cautiously describe the PRA as traversing a preparatory "people's democratic revolution" phase "during which conditions will be created" for progress toward "socialist change." They stress that the role of the MPLA-PT as a Marxist-Leninist party is to "embark on the path of socialist construction" (Manchkha 1983:76-77; see also Gromyko 1983 and 1984:18). Having been disappointed in earlier African experiences, the Soviets are careful not to overstate how far the MPLA may have progressed down that socialist path.

Anatoli Gromyko, head of the Africa Institute in Moscow, has described African states with a "socialist orientation" as falling within two categories. The first includes those where "power is wielded by mass revolutionary democratic parties, which adhere to revolutionary but at the same time petty-bourgeois ideology"—states like Algeria and Tanzania. The second, higher category is composed of states like Angola that are led by Marxist "vanguard" parties and are pressing for a "wider and more profound range of revolutionary transformations embracing all or almost all spheres of social life." Ideally, governments headed by these parties will fashion anti-imperialist foreign policies "based on the principles of proletarian internationalism and on the desire for close cooperation with the Soviet Union and other socialist states and with the world Communist and workers' movement" (1984: 12-13). Such are Soviet hopes, if not firm expectations, with regard to Angola.

In October 1976 President Neto signed a Treaty of Friendship and Cooperation in Moscow. It pledged Angola and the Soviet Union to mutual military cooperation in order to strengthen their respective defense capabilities (*Izvestia*, 10 October 1976). Soviet reconnaissance planes use Angolan airfields to stage routine surveillance flights over the south Atlantic, and Soviet naval vessels anchor conspicuously at allotted facilities in the Luanda harbor.* The Soviet military presence is limited and its strategic interests appear modest, and Soviet air and naval units have avoided direct confrontation with forces intruding from South Africa (see Remek 1984). But in geopolitical terms their presence enables the Soviets to project a regional influence. They have joined with others in training rebel forces of the South West Africa People's Organization (SWAPO) and the African National Congress (ANC) on southern African soil. Their presence could also have the ultimate effect of increasing prospects of a serious superpower confrontation in the region if and as the political situation continues to deteriorate in racially divided South Africa.

From the MPLA's vantage point, the Soviet presence is indispensable. Confronted by a disciplined and well-armed insurgent force of some 15,000 UNITA soldiers (plus as many local militia) and subject to repeated incursions by the South African Defense Force interdicting or retaliating against SWAPO raids from Angolan bases into South African-administered Namibia, the MPLA is utterly dependent for survival on its Communist allies.

Supplied by a fleet of two to three hundred South African-fueled trucks plying the rutted tracks leading north from the vicinity of UNITA's thatched hut "capital" of Jamba in the southeast corner of the country to the Benguela railroad and beyond, Savimbi's guerrillas have been constrained only by a lack of airpower from taking and holding major population centers. Boasting external funding of some $60-70 million annually from Arab and other sources (*Washington Post*, 28 August 1984), Savimbi has successfully defied all MPLA efforts to eliminate him and his movement. In

---

*These facilities are presumably not considered to be "foreign military bases," the installation of which is specifically prohibited by the PRA constitution.

concert with South African action, UNITA has forced the PRA to spend half or more of its oil revenue for defense and security.

Beginning in 1978, periodic South African incursions into southern Angola complemented UNITA expansion up the eastern side of the country to force the PRA to increase expenditures on sophisticated Soviet weaponry. Accordingly, the PRA has felt obliged to acquire Mig 21s and 23s, Mi-24 helicopter gunships, mobile radar installations, anti-aircraft vehicles and guns, and tanks, heavy artillery, armored cars, and trucks by the hundreds (accompanied by Soviet, East German, and Cuban pilots and technicians). The Angolans pay in hard currency for most of these arms, although in 1984, in the wake of intensified South African/UNITA pressure, the Soviets reportedly eased and lengthened the terms of payment. The Angolans are also obliged to pay for the supplies and maintenance (but they claim not the salaries) of Cuba's expeditionary force.

Prolonged, indecisive UNITA insurgency serves Soviet interests. It assures the USSR of significant arms sales, continued MPLA military dependency, and thus Soviet regional presence, and above all it undermines American diplomatic efforts to reduce cross-boundary conflict and promote negotiated solutions to explosive political tensions throughout southern Africa. UNITA's "anti-Communist" insurgency along with South Africa's rejection of an internationally sanctioned Namibian settlement that might bring an allegedly "pro-Communist" SWAPO to power, runs counter to real and declared American interest in fostering political accommodations that could lead to a deescalation of violence and a withdrawal of foreign troops (Cubans from Angola and South Africans from Namibia). The failure of the American government to persuade South Africa either to forego its "destabilization" policies of cross-boundary military attacks and support for UNITA insurgency or to accept a Western-backed formula for a political settlement in Namibia has left the Soviet Union and Cuba firmly ensconced as the guarantors of PRA survival.

Unable to hold towns in the face of assaults by Soviet-built aircraft, UNITA nonetheless seems capable of pursuing a destructive, no-win insurgency almost indefinitely. Should UNITA ever make good on threats to take the war to the streets of Luanda, it seems likely, as Western diplomats suggest, that the Soviets and Cubans would simply "up the stake" (*New York Times*, 28 August 1984). On the other hand, whether out of prudent deference to South Africa, or a long-term strategy that counts on ultimate marginalization, demoralization, and fragmentation to reduce UNITA, or a more cynical calculation that continued UNITA insurgency serves the cause of consolidating Soviet influence, or technical problems of military targeting and coordination, or some combination of these reasons, as of early 1986 the Soviets had still not acted to enable the Angolan airforce to strike against UNITA's truck convoys or its political nerve center of Jamba.

The Soviets have engaged their prestige in Angola, however, to a greater degree than they ever did in such "African socialist" states as Ghana and Guinea. Their political, ideological, and military investment in Angola covers a span of nearly three decades. In the MPLA, they may perceive that they have finally found an African political organization whose Marxist roots and experience of armed insurgency, along with Soviet mentoring, have caused it to make a serious commitment to "scientific socialism." When President Jose Eduardo dos Santos visited Moscow in May 1983, Soviet Communist party leader Yuri Andropov pointedly welcomed the steadfastness ("invariable course") of the MPLA in "defending revolutionary gains and creating the foundations of a socialist society." In return for this, he pledged continuing Soviet commitment to "the defense of [the PRA's] sovereignty, independence, and territorial integrity" (*Pravda*, 21 May 1983).

ANGOLA'S FUTURE ORIENTATION

Is Angola fated to a future of Soviet-style as well as Soviet-protected Marxist-Leninist rule? Though no one within the party leadership openly questions the MPLA's socialist option, even senior Marxists such as Lara accept that the details, the specific qualities of Angolan socialism, have yet to be determined. The character of Angolan socialism, they say, will be worked out in an interactive, internal process of debate and experience. It will not be dictated from outside.

Some political indicators point toward a Soviet style of governance. MPLA leaders categorically reject the Western concept of political pluralism, defend the party policy of denying membership to religious "believers," and hold that policy debate must stay within the parameters of Marxism-Leninism (as interpreted by Angolans at any given time). Angolan media are party-controlled. Luanda's only newspaper, the *Jornal de Angola*, is a party organ. Radio and television beam an exhortative stream of MPLA political messages (presented in the upbeat style of American commercials). The only available foreign press is Soviet and Cuban.

On the other hand, all this has not precluded the official Angolan Writers' Union, under the direction of noted Angolan author Luandino Vieira (*Luuanda* and *The Real Life of Domingos Xavier*) from becoming a center of uninhibited intellectual exchange. Free-flowing discussion within the Writers' Union suggests that Angolan cultural life may be relatively open and tolerant so long as it is allowed to develop free from the external ideological dictate that might result from sustained dependence on Soviet and Cuban military support.

The prevailing nationalist tone of the Writers' Union was set by the PRA's founding president, Agostinho Neto. A physician-poet, Neto was passionately concerned with intellectual matters. In key policy statements made to the governing body of the Writers' Union in 1977 and 1979, he called for a liberal definition of what constituted legitimate subject matter for Angolan authors. Angolan literature, he said, should reflect Angolan culture as it is, blemishes and all. It should describe or caricature the "petty bourgeoisie" and not just exalt peasants and workers (1979: 12).

Asserting the importance of Angolan cultural expression (including the use of ethnic languages), Neto rejected the imposition of a literary dogma such as Soviet "socialist realism." The Angolan Writers' Union (the sole vehicle for publication), he urged, "should not fall into fixed patterns or stereotypes like those of the socialist realist theorists." Angolan writers should draw upon external techniques only when fully "in possession of an Angolan cultural heritage." Pursuing his nationalist theme but using Marxist terminology, he continued, "We have not yet reached a level of material production that will permit us to dedicate ourselves intensively to spiritual production. We need more time. But, Comrade Writers, that time cannot be taken up with accommodations to imported themes and forms." In its quest for a national culture, Angola must encourage "the broadest possible debate on ideas" and foster research on and public presentation of all forms of culture "without any preconceived notions of an artistic or linguistic nature" (1979: 26-68).

Agostinho Neto seemed to be signaling that cultural pluralism, as distinct from political pluralism, should be condoned. But could the two be separated? The largely frustrated desire of Angolan writers and academics to establish contact and interchange with the

Western world highlights the tensions between cultural pluralism and political uniformity. While the young psychologist-rector of the University of Angola, Dr. João Filipe Martins, has lobbied for increased funding, broad external contacts and academic freedom, the MPLA Secretary for Information, Roberto de Almeida, one of the veteran MPLA leaders influenced by the bitter years of exile and perceived Western hostility, has pressed for adherence to a "correct" political line by instructors and instructional materials in the university.

Mixed signals within official ideology are nowhere more apparent than in the statements of President dos Santos. His 1985 statements on economic policy constitute a case in point. Speaking to a party conference, he acknowledged the failure of past agricultural policies and stressed the need for a new approach to rural development. But he also stressed a need to fight "liberalism" and "individualism" and to prevent the emergence of a "rural bourgeoisie" whose development could endanger the "consolidation" of a worker-peasant alliance (dos Santos 1985a).

The "Declaration of the MPLA-PT on the Tenth Anniversary of the People's Republic of Angola" is similarly ambiguous:

> Our country's experiences teach us that the path to economic progress is very complex, and they prove the modernity of Lenin's words that the classes which are oppressed and kept in the claws of misery and ignorance through violence cannot carry out a revolution without errors. With everyone aware of this need for self-criticism and goodwill to amend errors, the task of consolidating the centralized leadership of the economy becomes doubly important, as does the consistent implementation of the fundamental principle of the socialist leadership—that is, unity of orientation, execution, and control (MPLA-PT 1985).

Whether future emphasis will be placed on the themes of "centralized leadership" and "control" or, contrastingly, on themes of "self-criticism" and "goodwill" remains to be seen. The Second Congress of the MPLA-PT, which met in December 1985, suggests a significant, ongoing evolution in party thinking. Intra-party policy debate and elections at local and provincial levels leading up to the congress prepared the way for reappraisal and change. Calling for "realistic" economic policies, the party concluded that systems of family and small private enterprise beginning to develop in Angola's agricultural sector might appropriately be extended to other sectors of modest technology. It endorsed regulated competition among legalized private traders as potentially beneficial and less threatening to the country's "socialist option" than prevalent black market trading "outside the law." Exercising critical political judgment, it removed Lara (presumably held responsible for deficiencies in party organization) and other veteran mestiço leaders from the highest organs of the party and replaced them with black political and military associates of President dos Santos—for example, Foreign Minister Alfonso Van Dúnem "Mbinda" (dos Santos 1985b; de Almeida 1986: xvi).

Western hopes that a young, emerging technocratic elite might gradually gain ascendancy over "doctrinaire party veterans" and lead to economic and even political liberalization accordingly gained credibility. Some MPLA leaders reportedly even went so far as to propose a policy of "national reconciliation" that would bring long-time political opponents (with the exception of an arch foe like Savimbi) into a supragovernmental council designed to attract dissidents away from bush insurgency and exile, incorporate new talent within the thin ranks of public administration, and hasten an end to internal conflict (*Jeune Afrique* [Paris], no. 1258, 13 February 1985: 55). So long as insecurity and destruction occasioned by continuing war perpetuate military dependency on the Soviets and Cubans, however, hard-line opponents of the "appeasement of traitors" seem likely to block such sweeping political accommodation.

In a move that threatened to increase the pressures of war, press the MPLA into a greater dependence on the Soviets and Cubans, and possibly even reverse the course of evolving economic and political change, the United States announced in early 1986 that it intended to provide military assistance to UNITA. Seemingly having failed to persuade South Africa to accept an international settlement for Namibia that could open the way to a phased withdrawal of Cuban forces from Angola, the American government responded positively to importuning by South Africa, UNITA, and domestic political groups, who warned that advances made by Soviet-equipped and Cuban-backed Angolan forces in 1985 might presage a decisive air and tank assault on UNITA strongholds in southeastern Angola in 1986. In February 1986 Assistant Secretary of State for African Affairs Chester A. Crocker informed the Senate Committee on Foreign Relations that the Reagan administration had decided to provide UNITA with anti-tank and anti-aircraft weapons (*New York Times*, 19 February 1986). The MPLA, he said, had "sought to reverse two years of UNITA gains" and to deal a "death blow" to that movement. "They failed. It is important in our view that they continue to fail" (Crocker 1986).

President dos Santos warned that American assistance to anti-government rebels would force him to solicit additional aid from the MPLA's "traditional friends"—the Soviet Union, Cuba, and other socialist countries (Angolan News Agency [Lisbon], 9 January 1986). The American government, nevertheless, apparently calculated that reinforced military pressure in conjunction with falling world oil prices would force a war-weary Angolan government to negotiate with Savimbi and agree to the departure of most, if not all, Cuban troops. Its calculations attached more importance to a show of American "power" than to MPLA distrust of Savimbi's ambitions and ties to South Africa or to widespread conjecture that the MPLA knew, as did Savimbi, that if brought into the government, he would probably "eat his coalition partners, politically, for breakfast" (*The Economist* [London], 1 February 1986: 16). The MPLA was left with the (also risky) alternative of pressing ahead in quest of a clear-cut military victory, the hopes for which would depend upon costly, sophisticated Soviet weaponry and Cuban backup forces.

The United States seemed to be acting out of frustration with the failure of its diplomatic efforts to produce timely, definitive results. It refused to acknowledge a relationship between "greater Soviet involvement" and two years of "gains" by (South African-assisted) UNITA insurgents (Crocker 1986). In the process of using military power to tip the scales of Angola's bipolar dependency away from the Soviet Union and to force "negotiated resolutions in southern Africa," however, it could find itself, as in 1975, having to choose between massive support for besieged and intertwined UNITA and South African forces or a humiliating, self-inflicted political defeat. Because of an impatient disregard for long-term trends coupled with a demand for short-term payoffs, American policy might serve to arouse old anti-American animosities and push the MPLA into a more pro-Soviet orientation. To pursue such a policy would reflect little understanding of the causes and dynamics of Angola's bipolar dependency. One could only hope, instead, that increased awareness of the risks inherent in a bipolar collision of great and small powers in Angola would give rise to diplomatic initiatives and responses sufficiently bold and inventive to rescue Angola from the externally armed violence that has ravaged it for a quarter of a century.

MARXISM-LENINISM IN ETHIOPIA:
POLITICAL IMPASSE AND ECONOMIC DETERIORATION

Paul B. Henze

The changes in government which led to the Ethiopian Revolution during the momentous year 1974 did not arise from a massive upwelling of peasant discontent. Nor was urban unrest more than an incidental factor. Military restiveness was at least as important. The key factor that caused a series of nonviolent protest actions to evolve into a revolutionary situation was the inability of the imperial regime to respond to stress.* In large part this was a failure of Emperor Haile Selassie I, who had provided dynamic leadership for nearly fifty years. His style of leadership was far from dictatorial, but it was paternalistic and mildly authoritarian. Even the "young technocrats"— men with modern education, often acquired or completed abroad, who had become prominent in the middle levels of government during the 1960s—were accustomed to depending on the emperor for initiative and reluctant to take major decisions on their own. The traditional governing classes, revolutionary events proved, had lost much of their capacity to mobilize and act in a time of crisis. The political orientation of both the modern and traditional leadership elements was vertical. There was very little subgroup cohesion or class consciousness. Haile Selassie, nearing eighty-two, had postponed reorganizing and reinvigorating his government until it was too late. He kept the same prime minister for almost sixteen years. Thus the imperial regime fell victim to a combination of problems none of

---

*I have discussed the causes of the Ethiopian Revolution in several earlier works; for example, see Henze (1985). The best available analysis of the imperial system in Ethiopia remains Clapham (1969).

The views expressed herein are entirely those of the author and do not represent the judgment of the Rand Corporation.

which in themselves, singly or together, would have constituted an unmanageable challenge just a few years before.*

Haile Selassie's government had neither been notably corrupt nor, by Third World standards, particularly oppressive. As discontent began to be expressed openly in early 1974, the characteristic government response was half-hearted attempts at conciliation and hurried promises of reform. The military was not employed against the civil population. Violence was exceptional. Ministerial changes, once the process began, followed each other so quickly that no governing team had a chance to consolidate its position or even formulate a coherent response to the growing—but not very radical— demands for accelerated change. The revolutionary process was remarkably good-natured well beyond the point where a bewildered Haile Selassie was bundled into a Volkswagen on the eve of the Ethiopian New Year in September 1974 and driven away from his palace to imprisonment. There was no visible outside interference in Ethiopian affairs as the revolution gained momentum. We can say this for certain as far as the West is concerned, for the Ethiopian Revolution occurred at a time when the country's principal supporting power, the United States, was immobilized by the Watergate crisis and defeat in Vietnam. If there was clandestine interference from the East—a subject on which we lack concrete information—it was modest in scale and confined to the giving of political advice, and did not include the supply of arms or exertion of other forms of pressure.† Eastern influence need not be postulated to explain the abrupt turn toward Marxism-Leninism which occurred when the Provisional Military Administrative Committee (PMAC, more commonly known by the newly coined Amharic term, the Derg) took power from the imperial government and a few weeks later, largely as a result of its own internal differences, fell into crisis and executed fifty-nine officials of the former government. When the

---

*In 1960 the Imperial Bodyguard revolted while Haile Selassie was on a visit to Brazil, but he returned immediately and took charge decisively. No comprehensive account of the events of 1974 has yet been written. By far the best analysis of the early revolutionary period is Ottaway and Ottaway (1978).

†Rumors nevertheless abound of contacts between East European embassies in Addis Ababa and Derg members during the summer and fall of 1974. Lack of confirmation cannot be taken as proof that no such contacts occurred. The subject must remain open.

Ethiopian Revolution turned sharply leftward, it also turned bloody. Blood has never stopped flowing since.*

THE REVOLUTIONARY JUNTA

The Derg was a hurriedly organized group which operated in highly secretive fashion from the very beginning. It was rent with factionalism. Maj. Mengistu Haile Mariam remained in the background until early 1977 but was identified early as one of the Derg's most energetic and ruthless members. We still know too little about this man to judge what went into the formation of his basic political outlook and why he displayed such an early and strong aversion to the United States and to Western democratic principles. Before any prerequisites for a socialist system had been created in Ethiopia, Mengistu became an uncompromising advocate of "Ethiopian Socialism," which seemed to have both Russian and Chinese features.† The main appeal of "socialism" to him and his closest associates may have been simply that it justified military dictatorship in the name of the people without requiring the Derg to risk its often precarious hold on power by resorting to any concrete arrangements to present its new government as the people's choice. Imperial Ethiopia had a well-defined, functioning constitutional structure and a parliamentary system that could have been exploited to create the framework for an East European-type "people's democracy." The Derg confined this structure to the trash heap of history without a moment's hesitation. No nationwide "people's congress" was called to confer legitimacy on the PMAC's rule. Not even sham elections were held. No new constitution was drafted. When, after a long delay and a great deal of Soviet pressure, a Marxist-Leninist Vanguard Party (MLVP) was finally proclaimed in September 1984 on the tenth anniversary of the deposition of Haile Selassie, the title

---

*Eritrean policy appears to have been the most contentious issue provoking bloodshed. For a more detailed discussion of this period, see Erlich (1983:43-54).

†I have discussed Ethiopian socialism at greater length in Henze (1985:10-16). Lefort (1983) offers an extensive discussion of the nature of Ethiopian socialism.

Provisional Military Government of Socialist Ethiopia, was still in use.*

In spite of some early similarities with Chinese Communist practice, there is no serious evidence of Chinese Communist influence on the Ethiopian Revolution or orientation toward China by any significant Derg faction.† The elements in the Derg that kept coming out on top in the frequent bloody confrontations that occurred through 1977 clearly opted for Soviet-style socialism and a strong Moscow orientation. The elements within the military that kept losing out (and usually paying with their lives) seem almost invariably to have favored a more nonaligned position or some degree of rapprochement to the West. Evidently important Derg elements— including Mengistu—expected that adopting a Soviet-style social, political, and economic system would accelerate—and ensure— development of a close strategic relationship with the Soviet Union. This was a naive expectation and oversimplified the task of reorientation from long-standing Western relationships. Such an attitude also failed to take into account the factors which had to influence Soviet judgments on how power could be consolidated throughout the whole Horn/South Arabian region.** While—as the events of 1977 proved—the Soviets recognized Ethiopia as the pivotal country and greatest political prize in the region, their basic political conservatism prevented them from hastily jettisoning the large investment they had made in Somalia starting in the early 1960s. Indeed their most significant initial response to the Ethiopian Revolution was a rapid expansion of military aid to Somalia, fulfilling the promise of a full client relationship inherent in the signing of a Friendship Treaty with President Mohamed Siad Barre in 1974. They did not abandon support of the Eritrean insurgency until 1976, and they probably contributed clandestinely to the political ferment that came close to undermining

---

*A series of pseudonymous articles has been published in the *Journal of Northeast African Studies* (East Lansing, Mich.) during the past several years, of which the most recent, "The Lives and Times of the Dergue" (5, 3 [1984]:1-42), provides perhaps the best comment and analysis available on the workings and membership of this always mysterious body, whose methods of operation are still shrouded in secrecy. There is as yet little reason to believe that the Ethiopian Workers' Party has replaced, or was ever intended to replace, the Derg (see below).

†The Soviets have repeatedly accused the Chinese of supporting dissident as well as separatist movements in Ethiopia; for example, see Gromyko, ed. (1981).

**I have discussed these factors at greater length in Henze (1983b).

the Derg's hold on power during 1976-77 by supporting rival parties simultaneously to see which might prove most effective.*

The Derg's radical reforms and the confusion that arose from efforts to form a political movement to implement socialism almost destroyed the Derg's capacity to govern and sparked serious factionalism within the ruling junta itself. Yet the structural changes which the Derg implemented in the imperial government bureaucracy were more rhetorical than real. Most of the institutions and agencies of the imperial regime and a substantial portion of imperial civil servants remained in place and kept the government and economy functioning. The Derg members, all inexperienced in the management of governing processes, may thus have misled themselves about the ease with which their new system could be imposed on the population. Moreover, Derg power was often weak in outlying parts of the country. It was never effectively established in parts of the north. Rival political groupings gained backing from factions in the Derg, and this factionalism was reflected in provincial government. It is no wonder that Siad Barre, confident of Moscow support, concluded that Ethiopia was disintegrating and planned to attack, shatter the Derg's control, and seize coveted territories. It is impossible that the Soviets, with over 4,000 advisers in Somalia by 1977, were unaware of Siad's plans—if in fact they did not encourage him.†

Siad Barre miscalculated badly, saved the Derg, and forced the Soviets to make a choice they wished to avoid. This, in brief, is what happened in the critical watershed year 1977. A dramatic Soviet air- and sealift in November 1977—including the dispatch of 18,000 Cubans to fight the Somalis—the provision of vast quantities of equipment to arm the hastily expanded Ethiopian military forces, and the direct involvement of senior Soviet and Cuban generals in managing military operations brought Ethiopia into a close strategic relationship with Moscow. Kremlin leaders had hoped for a simpler and less costly resolution of the contradictions into which their assertive policies in the Horn of Africa had brought them and one that would have ensured Soviet hegemony in the entire Horn region. Fidel Castro had been sent on an urgent tour of all Horn capitals as well as Aden in March 1977 to try to effect a federation of the entire

---

*I have discussed this period at greater length in Henze (1981:55-74).

†This subject is discussed at length in Henze (1983b), as well as Henze (1983a:150-86).

area, into which both the Eritrean and Ogaden conflicts could be subsumed. He failed.*

EFFORTS TO IMPLEMENT SOCIALISM

In some respects the implementation of socialism in revolutionary Ethiopia was rapid—almost precipitate. In others it was very slow. The result is a very mixed picture. Initial measures in 1975 included extensive nationalization of private enterprises (especially those owned by foreign interests), sweeping rural land reform which was actually *nationalization* of all agricultural land, and urban land reform, which resulted in effect in the confiscation and nationalization of most privately owned rental property. During this same period the Derg moved decisively against labor unions, professional associations, and most voluntary welfare and service groups, replacing them with Communist-style organizations under direct state control. The follow-up to these initial moves was often far from thorough or efficient, however. Banking was not immediately nationalized. Many small- and medium-scale private industrial and commercial establishments were permitted to continue. Eventually policy shifted to attempts to attract foreign investment, but with little response from potential investors. The Derg's authoritarian methods, the secrecy of its decision-making processes, and its ideological pronouncements— invariably reflecting Soviet-style approaches to political and economic management—left little doubt among the population of the Derg's ultimate intentions: to create in Ethiopia a classic Soviet-style people's democracy.†

Initial positive responses to land reform from peasants in central and southern parts of the country soon turned into resistance to

---

*Castro is reported to have declared that none of the leaders in the area understood the primacy of socialism over nationalism. Mengistu apparently proved the most difficult to deal with, for acceptance of the formula Castro was advocating would have meant a de facto partition of Ethiopia, giving both Eritrea and the Ogaden separate status. Siad Barre was more pleased with Castro, awarding him the Great Star of Somalia during this visit.

†Ottaway and Ottaway (1978) provide the most detail on the implementation of Ethiopian socialism during this period. For a discussion of these developments with little criticism and lavish praise, see Schwab (1985). Schwab had the misfortune to complete this sycophantic work before a famine crisis in late 1984 exposed all the revolutionary regime's shortcomings and failures.

steps aimed to encourage—and force—collectivization. In the north land reform was less consistently implemented; when applied, it frequently met with strong resistance. Almost all former commercial and large-scale private farms were turned into state farms. Results were generally poor, for even when productivity was maintained, costs and manpower skyrocketed. Derg policy has nevertheless continued to encourage Soviet-style organization of agriculture, though little concrete progress toward collectivization has been made. Regulations forbidding the hiring of labor and consolidation or exchange of allocated land have reminded peasants that they are state tenants, not owners. The state has discriminated against individual peasants in both crass and subtle ways. Purchasing policies— designed to keep prices low—and a lack of consumer goods to buy with earnings from agricultural produce have discouraged production. Continued nationalization of some of the most important specialized areas of agricultural activity—for example, the coffee trade (coffee is Ethiopia's primary export commodity)—have driven a substantial share of the country's most productive agricultural export activity underground.*

Several of Ethiopia's large-scale public corporations—the Power Authority, the Highway Authority, and Ethiopian Airlines—could not be nationalized because they were already state enterprises with on the whole a good record of efficiency and dynamism during the imperial period. (Eritreans played—and have continued to play—an important role in most of these organizations.) These organizations have to a remarkable degree been successful in maintaining their autonomy and avoiding Derg interference. Many of them have retained a sizable proportion of their professional manpower. The most striking example of independence is Ethiopian Airlines, originally established in 1946 as an affiliate of TWA. By the time of the revolution almost all its managerial and technical personnel were Ethiopian. Only a few advisers from Boeing and TWA were retained, and most of these departed during the first years of the revolution. Nevertheless, the airline maintained close Western connections and

---

*Agriculture accounted for half of Ethiopia's GDP and 90 percent of its exports in 1983. By 1981 per capita food production (on the basis of earlier population estimates which were revised upward by approximately 30 percent after the partial census of 1984) had already fallen to 84 percent of its 1970 level. The best available discussion of the critical situation in Ethiopian agriculture is Cohen (1984).

even during the period of maximum revolutionary commotion (1976-78) was able to adhere to high performance and maintenance standards. In recent years it has reached unprecedented levels of profitability and has been able to secure credit to purchase advanced U.S. and Canadian aircraft (two Boeing 767s in 1984, e.g.). Thus although it is a state corporation in a socialist economy, Ethiopian Airlines is in effect a successful capitalist enterprise operating according to U.S. management principles and resisting political interference.

As coffee earnings have fallen and other sources of export income have failed to materialize, and as the country's balance of payments situation has steadily worsened (foreign currency reserves were said to have dropped below $20 million at the end of 1984 but rose to over $100 million in 1985 as a result of customs charges on food and supplies brought in to alleviate famine), the Derg has been driven to seek new sources of foreign exchange. Tourism was selected as a priority area for development in the early 1980s. The approach was dogmatically socialist, however, with all hotels and resort facilities nationalized and all formerly private touring companies nationalized and amalgamated into a cumbersome National Tourist Organization. Scarce funds were invested in hotel expansion but have brought no significant return. The famine crisis which developed at the end of 1984 made the concept of rapid tourism development incongruous.

Even before spreading famine was acknowledged to be a serious national problem, the Derg had been attempting to force most agricultural trade and food supply services into a rigid, doctrinaire socialist mold. Urban neighborhood associations (*kebeles*) and rural peasant associations were given responsibility for the distribution of many staple foods at low (in effect subsidized) prices. Though both inefficient and susceptible to corruption, the system has been extended as a response to famine. Grain trade has been subjected to procurement price ceilings. The state grain corporation has been unable to handle the entire procurement process, however, with the result that half of the trading in grain is still done by private traders. These are hedged in by regulations which encourage corruption and inefficiency. In every respect socialist intervention in the economy has created greatly expanded bureaucracy, lowered efficiency, and consequently forced higher service costs. Both producers and consumers have been driven into a steadily expanding underground economy. While Ethiopia grew economically at an average annual rate of 5-7 percent during the decade preceding the revolution, growth since 1974 has averaged less than 2 percent per year and in 1984-85 probably ceased entirely.*

Politically the implementation of socialism should have led to the rapid formation of an MLVP. In theory this was anticipated as early as 1975, but the process was botched badly, with the result that a whole series of parties and rival groups, all radical, competed for influence on the Derg as well as among the population and created near chaos during 1976 and 1977. Many crosscurrents were reflected in the Derg itself. A key problem was tension that developed between Marxist intellectuals—for the most part returnees from exile in Europe and America—and the more pragmatic and power-conscious military officers who predominated in the Derg. Mengistu, who assumed open leadership of the revolution after Provisional Head of State Gen. Teferi Banti and several others were killed in a Derg shootout in February 1977, proved wary of intellectuals who thought they should play a dominant role in the revolutionary government and that soldiers should step aside. For their part, the intellectuals displayed an extraordinary lack of skill in organizational discipline and political maneuvering. The Red Terror of the winter of 1977-78 brought most of this political commotion to a bloody end and left Mengistu and his associates firmly in charge but with little desire for further adventures with political parties of any kind. The Committee for Organizing the Workers' Party of Ethiopia (COPWE) was finally set up in response to heavy Soviet pressure in December 1979. Nearly five years passed before it was formally transformed into a party. In its initial stages it was little more than a propaganda device. Even since its formal transformation into a party its membership remains small (30,000-40,000) and consists almost entirely of civil servants and military personnel. Far from being a leading element in the revolution, it is a tool of the Derg. The Derg itself has steadily shrunk in size. Ethiopian revolutionary leadership rests with Mengistu, who has adopted a more imperial style, and a small group of loyalists around him (see Henze 1984a).

Marxism-Leninism was a fad among students and young intellectuals in Ethiopia in the late 1960s and early 1970s, encouraged by Ethiopian student organizations operating from Europe and

---

*World Bank studies continue to be the best source of comprehensive data and professional judgments on the Ethiopian economy. They are reflected in the bank's annual *World Development Reports*.

North America; it was never seriously studied and put down no self-sustaining roots. Neither the peasantry nor city dwellers (most of them only a generation or two away from rural life) developed a serious interest in socialism. For the overwhelming majority of the population modernization was seen as naturally occurring along Western lines. Thus when "Ethiopian socialism" was proclaimed by the Derg as its guiding principle, it had little meaning to the population. Intellectuals who had returned from abroad in hopes of taking over the political leadership of the revolution were strongly influenced by various kinds of Western socialism in addition to Marxism-Leninism. None of them had any practical political experience. They found it difficult to relate to the dominant elements in the Derg, whom they often treated superciliously. Mengistu was little interested in the ideological formulations of these people and had no respect for them as practical manipulators of the levers of power. Thus in a country which had maintained its independence for millennia in the midst of external threats and among a people naturally gifted in political maneuvering—bargaining, challenge, compromise—a situation developed where the most active elements in political life were characterized by amateurishness and naivete.*

It is not surprising that revolutionary Ethiopia has displayed no creativity in elaborating or applying Marxism-Leninism to a highly distinct Third World society. The ideological level of political publications in Ethiopia has been low, the teaching of Marxism-Leninism in political indoctrination courses perfunctory. Confronted with great difficulties consolidating its control over outlying parts of the country, the Derg has been unable to give priority to the formulation of a body of ideology specially adapted to Ethiopian circumstances and traditions. These have nevertheless made themselves felt in many ways. A major element in Marxist-Leninist doctrine as it has been applied in countries as divergent as the USSR, China, and Yugoslavia—nationalities policy—has been of no assistance to the Derg in dealing with the multiple insurgencies that challenge its rule. Only the scantiest lip service has been paid to the notion that the country should be reorganized on nationalities lines. Most ironic has been the fact that the dominant leaders in the most persistent regional insurgencies—those of the Eritreans and Tigreans—claim to be more genuine Marxist-Leninists than Mengistu.†

*The best available collection of revolutionary documents is Moffa (1980).

†Numerous publications of the Eritrean and Tigrean Popular Liberation Fronts (EPLF and TPLF) make this claim. The EPLF program is printed verbatim in Davidson, Cliffe, and Selassie, eds. (1980:143-50).

A TURN TO THE EAST

The Derg's rapid declarative turn toward the East at the end of 1974 was greeted with enthusiasm by the Soviets and some of their East European client states as well as Cuba, but it did not result in a strategic reorientation. Ethiopia remained dependent upon the United States for the major portion of its military aid for the next two and a half years. Indeed American military aid was supplied at a much higher level *after* the revolution than it had been during the imperial period. In addition, the Derg inherited a treasury sufficiently well provided to make possible substantial military purchases— also from the United States. The United States continued economic assistance programs as well and encouraged expanded economic assistance by its European allies and a wide range of international lending agencies. The nationalization of U.S. and other Western investments (those of Italy and Holland were much larger than those of the United States) provoked no retaliation.* The United States continued to be Ethiopia's best export customer, taking a major portion of the annual coffee crop. Western advisers, including missionaries, remained active in many sectors of Ethiopian life during the first years following the revolution. However, a distinct coolness toward the West had been apparent in the Derg even before it took full power. There was very little contact with Western embassies, no travel to the United States or Europe by Derg members following the assumption of power, and a great deal of suspicion toward the Western press and Western intellectuals. Gradually Ethiopians who had had close Western associations found themselves discriminated against in both subtle and direct ways. The secretiveness of the Derg always made it difficult to ascertain just what its guiding principles were on such matters. We hear a good deal even today about alleged Western rejection of the Derg and hostility toward the revolution. Such accusations have a self-serving character and serve as ex post facto justification for the effects of the Derg's own approach. They are not borne out by examination of what happened at the time. Deteriorating security conditions in many parts of the country

---

*I refer here to the period immediately following the nationalizations. U.S. laws, which were applied by the Carter administration only after prolonged attempts to secure progress (not necessarily solution) toward settlement of nationalization claims, finally necessitated the termination of U.S. developmental aid in 1979.

during 1975 caused many resident foreigners, whether official or private, to feel apprehensive about their situation, and many who did not have diplomatic status left.

Early Derg political and ideological warmth toward the East brought an influx of visiting delegations and more diplomatic activity and receptivity toward Eastern propaganda, which soon dominated the state-controlled media. A short period of relative press freedom in 1974 was quickly brought to an end. There was no obvious pressure on the Soviets for economic or military assistance, however, nor (as far as we know) were they confronted with complaints about their sharply increased military aid to Somalia. Instead, somewhat incongruously, the United States was urged to increase military assistance to help counter the growing Somali threat. Soviet-friendly countries, including Cuba, continued to aid the Eritreans until 1976. Cuba did not move rapidly onto the Ethiopian scene and until early 1977 put far greater effort into assisting the Somalis.

As Mengistu consolidated his power in the Derg, it became more obvious that he aspired to a close strategic relationship with Moscow. Nevertheless, a sharp break in military orientation was clearly impractical. Mengistu would thus have welcomed military assistance from the Soviets while continuing to receive it from the Americans. There was no enthusiasm among the Ethiopian military for a shift to Soviet equipment, however. F-5E planes which were delivered on U.S. Secretary of State Henry Kissinger's approval in 1976 (as part of a commitment originally made to Haile Selassie in 1973) were received with great satisfaction by the Ethiopian air force.*

Everything we know and can deduce from the events of the winter of 1976-77 supports the impression that the Soviets played a clever game on the crucial military issue. They refused to commit themselves until the outcome of the U.S. presidential election of 1976 was clear. In view of the Democratic Party's stance on Angola, they appear to have interpreted the Democratic victory of Jimmy Carter as greatly reducing the risk of a precipitate U.S. response to a forward move in Ethiopia. Their principal condition for becoming Ethiopia's main military supplier was the termination of the long-standing U.S.-Ethiopian special relationship, based on a 1953 treaty

---

*Halliday and Molyneux (1981) mistakenly assert that the F-5E planes were never delivered. They enabled the Ethiopian air force to halt an initial Somali offensive in the summer of 1977 and to obliterate the Soviet-supplied Somali air force.

about to expire. Rancor over human rights criticisms (which had begun during the Ford administration) gave Mengistu an excuse to expel the Military Aid and Assistance Group (MAAG) and several other components of the U.S. mission in Ethiopia in two successive steps in the spring of 1977, leaving only a skeleton embassy and economic aid mission.

By this time it was too late for Mengistu to fend off the assault which Siad Barre had for some time been preparing. As indicated, there is no serious evidence that the Soviets tried to dissuade the Somalis from their plans to attack. In the months that followed, both Mengistu and the Soviets were confronted with much more drastic challenges than either can have envisioned; concrete conditions for a Soviet-Ethiopian strategic relationship were worked out in the framework of a crisis that threatened the Derg's hold on power as well as the territorial integrity of the country. Until a late stage in this process Moscow attempted to maintain a strong position in both Somalia and Ethiopia and clearly aspired to gain hegemony over the entire Horn. When the speed and initial success of the Somali attack made this impossible, Moscow opted for Ethiopia over Somalia, but both Siad and the Soviets delayed a break as long as possible. Only when the Soviet air- and sealift began in 1977 did Siad Barre expel the Soviets and Cubans, many of whom went directly from Somalia to Ethiopia; however, Soviet-Somali diplomatic relations were never broken.*

The story of the dramatic rescue of Mengistu's regime—and full Soviet embrace of Mengistu himself—does not need to be repeated here, for its main outlines are well known. In early March 1978, when the Somalis had to admit defeat and withdraw the regular troops they claimed they had never had in Ethiopia, Siad Barre shifted to guerrilla operations, which represented an annoying challenge to the Ethiopians in the Ogaden and until 1980 prevented consolidation of a U.S.-Somali strategic relationship. Guerrilla warfare also exacerbated the Ogaden refugee problem, almost entirely at Somalia's expense. Though overshadowed now by the massive dislocations caused by fighting and famine in northern Ethiopia in 1984-85, this refugee problem has never been solved and stands as an appalling example of the kind of human suffering resulting from both countries' reliance on the Soviet Union.†

*See Henze (1983b) for a more detailed description of this sequence of developments.

†Henze (1982) provides detailed statistics and analysis of all arms and other

The Soviets had to pay a high price in weapons and transport to rescue the Ethiopian revolutionary government—$2 billion is a good estimate—and the Cubans a substantial price in manpower and loss of life. Heavy weapons deliveries have continued during the ensuing years but have not enabled the swollen Ethiopian army to prevail in Eritrea or elsewhere in the north, where the Derg's military position has steadily worsened since 1979, following an initially partially successful offensive in 1978. The exact amount of indebtedness the Ethiopian regime has incurred for Soviet weaponry and for the services of the Cubans is not publicly known. It is possible that conditions for repayment have never been agreed upon between the Derg and the Soviets. Heavy continuing local costs for maintaining the Cubans were a factor in reducing their numbers after mid-1983. Ethiopian indebtedness gives the Soviets some leverage over Mengistu, but there is no way an impoverished Ethiopia—increasingly strained by maintaining an army of more than 250,000 in the face of economic stagnation—can ever entirely repay this Soviet assistance.

During the first year following the defeat of the Somalis, there was overt evidence of strain in the Ethiopian-Soviet relationship, with the Cubans and South Yemenis getting into difficulties as well. Hasty efforts to force formation of a civilian-led MLVP, favoritism toward Marxist intellectuals whom Mengistu did not trust, and possibly disagreements over strategy in Eritrea and the Cuban role there resulted in departure of both the Cuban and Soviet ambassadors (and other personnel) in the summer of 1978 and the recall to Aden of the South Yemeni chargé. If Mengistu and his close supporters had any inclination to distance themselves from the close Soviet relationship into which the military rescue operation of 1977 had thrust them, these differences would have provided a convenient occasion. On the contrary, Mengistu seems to have desired to exploit the situation to get a closer relationship on his terms. Relations with Castro were quickly patched up, and in November 1978 a Friendship Treaty was signed in Moscow. Neither the Soviets nor the Cubans, in spite of their large presence in the country, were permitted to gain the kind of predominance that would have made Mengistu's hold on power directly dependent on them.* Subsequent difficulties are

forms of assistance supplied to Horn countries by all foreign donors and documents the impact of Soviet arms aid in exacerbating tensions among the countries of the region.

*A Ministry of State Security was established in August 1978, combining former separate security and intelligence elements which the Derg had not dis-

known to have developed not only over the slowness with which the MLVP was brought into existence (as noted, COPWE was not established until December 1979), but also over economic assistance.

Ethiopia proved of very little use to the USSR in pursuing its objectives in other parts of Africa and the Third World. In part this was the inevitable result of continued internal strain, which required all Ethiopian military manpower at home. It also reflected a deep Ethiopian tradition. The country has never aimed to interfere to any significant extent in the affairs of its neighbors, nor has it cherished ambitions of extending power and influence abroad. In this Mengistu is true to Ethiopian tradition.

While military dependence upon the Soviet Union has provided the Ethiopian revolutionary leadership with large-scale arms and training assistance that would otherwise be unobtainable, the Derg's sharp pro-Soviet orientation has tended to freeze (at best) or exacerbate all Ethiopia's foreign confrontations as well as its internal insurgencies. The problems of Soviet dependence and external/ internal strife are in many respects closely linked. The Soviet strategic relationship requires a permanent militarization of Ethiopian society and offers no promise of easing tensions with countries such as Somalia and Sudan. An inevitable result is the stagnation and degeneration of the Ethiopian economy. The food crisis which has attracted worldwide attention since the end of 1984 had been building up over several years. Drought was only a secondary cause. There can be little doubt that some elements in the regime hoped to starve out rebellious populations in Eritrea, Tigre, and elsewhere in the north. There was an almost mystic faith that the lavish celebrations of the tenth anniversary of the revolution would ease all of Ethiopia's increasingly pressing problems and perhaps very concrete expectations that the establishment of the Ethiopian Workers' Party would at last lead to an influx of Soviet and East European economic aid that would cause the famine to disappear. Instead everything went from bad to worse during the final months of 1984, and the regime stood condemned before the world for crassness and by its own people for ineptitude and blind adherence to discredited economic prescriptions.

banded when it replaced the imperial regime. Though reported to benefit from aid and advice from both the Soviet Union and East Germany, this ministry has remained firmly in Ethiopian hands and retains a large number of professional officers who held security positions in prerevolutionary times.

SYSTEMIC CRISIS

The revolutionary regime's confused response to the famine, from which it has been temporarily rescued by massive aid from the United States and the West in general, has exposed fundamental dilemmas and generated a systemic crisis from which no escape can be envisioned. Ethiopia's most fundamental need is self-sustained economic growth. The country is much more favorably endowed than much of Africa for broad agricultural development based on Green Revolution technology that is available only from the West and can be effectively applied only if favorable political, social, and economic circumstances are created. Marxist-Leninist prescriptions for agriculture have condemned Ethiopia to permanent agricultural decline. Almost no industrial growth has taken place since the revolution. As of this writing, however, the Derg has not yet decisively shifted course to apply the lessons that the famine demonstrates. Resettlement of rebellious and hunger-stricken Tigreans to the southwest, utilizing Soviet transport aircraft, has generated new dissension and hardship. Moreover, the population of Wollega, where resettlement has been concentrated, was alienated from the regime early in the revolution by the oppression of its indigenous church. Villagization in regions unaffected by famine has caused a new outflow of refugees to Somalia.*

The Soviets were able to execute a spectacular quick fix in 1977, which gave them great short-term strategic advantages, by shipping in arms and Cubans to save Mengistu from the consequences of the political and military disarray into which his amateurish and intemperate leadership had plunged the country in the first years of the revolution. No such quick fix can be envisioned now. The Soviets have little food to spare. They lack the resources and the know-how to help the Derg devise even short-term palliatives that will restore agricultural productivity. The massive famine relief operations have opened the country to Western personnel and expanded Western influence again; it will be difficult for the regime to resort to oppression to reduce the effects of this process. Not only has it lost credibility with a large portion of the population and its own officials, but it has also lost some of its ability to intimidate and

---

*This new refugee wave was the subject of extensive newspaper reporting in the spring of 1986. One of the most informative accounts appeared in the *Wall Street Journal*, 27 May 1986.

coerce. Reconciliation with Sudan offers some hope of reducing strains for both countries, as it did in 1972, but it will probably be less easy to achieve than when more skilled leaders (i.e., Gaafar Nimiery and Haile Selassie) were in charge.*

The ideology of the Derg has been discredited. The MLVP is of little relevance in the present critical situation. While deadlock and stagnation could persist in Ethiopia for months or perhaps years, this seems unlikely. In many ways Ethiopian nationalism has been strengthened by the revolutionary ordeal. It can now be seen to rest on more than a two thousand-year-old dynastic tradition. Religion has been strengthened—both Christianity and Islam—and the regime, whatever its ultimate intentions, cannot afford to challenge religion. Some of the regime's programs—such as a massive literacy campaign— have created expectations for modernization and progress that are broader and stronger than those which contributed to the original revolutionary ferment of 1974.

The strong pro-Soviet ideological and strategic orientation of the Ethiopian revolutionary leadership does not extend beyond the narrow group of Derg survivors who surround Mengistu. No pro-Soviet faction exists in Ethiopia. Socialism as a doctrine is equated in the minds of the population with hardship, insecurity, and bloodshed. Quite the opposite of an ideological, economic, or strategic reorientation is occurring. The reaction to the present impasse, once it bursts forth, is likely to be much more profoundly anchored in popular attitudes and readiness for commitment than was the 1974 revolutionary process.

---

*There was also a better basis for confidence between the two leaders and the two countries at that time, for neither had links with outside powers that appeared inimical to the interests of the other. Nimeiry had just broken off a close Soviet relationship after an attempt by the Sudan Communist Party to overthrow him. Though Israel, with which Ethiopia still had a close relationship, had aided the southern Sudanese rebellion, Ethiopia was in a position to convince Nimeiry that it would not permit resumption of such aid. Since Ethiopian-Sudanese strains then (as now) were entirely a function of external forces and neither country had (or has) any economic, political, or territorial claims on the other, there remains a natural basis for reconciliation. For it to be achieved, however, each government must have the strength and sense of security to convince the other of its ability to implement a genuine settlement.

MOZAMBIQUE: THE NKOMATI ACCORD

Martin Lowenkopf

Over the past fifteen years southern Africa has been the scene of increasing conflict and international concern. In 1975 longstanding insurgencies in Angola and Mozambique culminated, and the liberation process was speeded up in Rhodesia. Following a coup in Lisbon, Portugal yielded independence in its colonies to the groups it had been fighting, several of which had received aid from the Soviet Union. In Angola, Cuban troops repulsed a South African invasion and helped the Movimento Popular de Libertação de Angola (MPLA) to prevail over its internal rivals. The United States and Great Britain played key roles in negotiations leading to Zimbabwe's independence in 1980 under Robert Mugabe.

In 1977 the United States entered the Namibian imbroglio at the head of the so-called Western Contact Group (composed also of Canada and West European countries) in a quest for a peaceful transition to independence under UN Security Council Resolutions 385 (1976) and 435 (1978).* A guerrilla war launched from Angola embroiled the MPLA in direct conflict with South Africa. Cuban and Soviet military assistance to the MPLA grew substantially.

From South Africa's perspective, a net of hostile black regimes, several allied with the Soviet Union, was tightening around its borders. Guerrillas of the African National Congress (ANC), South Africa's militant adversary, were operating from a number of these states. Pretoria's response was to raise the level of confrontation and the costs to its neighbors of harboring the ANC. Cross-border assaults into Angola reached at times over two hundred miles into the country. Moreover, South Africa openly supported an anti-MPLA guerrilla movement that had carried its operations into central Angola

---

*Resolution 385, in calling for the withdrawal from Namibia of South Africa's "illegal" administration, warned that appropriate measures would be considered in the event of noncompliance. Resolution 435, which established a UN Transition Assistance Group (UNTAG), softened Resolution 385 by calling on South Africa to "cooperate with the Secretary General."

and by 1985 to the gates of Luanda. As we will see, it pursued a similar course of action against Mozambique (as well as Lesotho and, to a lesser extent, Botswana).

All the signs pointed to a further escalation of regional violence when on 16 March 1984, Mozambique and South Africa signed a nonaggression pact known as the Nkomati Accord. At a stroke, Mozambique signaled its intention to shift from a posture of overt hostility to South Africa—it had been harboring and helping the ANC—and seemed to be modifying, if not abandoning, its self-avowed Marxist-Leninist course by reopening its economy to South African and Western investment and aid. By its accession to the accord, South Africa turned from trying to overthrow the regime of Samora Machel to supporting it. These turnabouts may make the Nkomati Accord the transcendent political event of the 1980s in southern Africa. (The complete text of the Nkomati Accord is presented in the appendix.)

Under the accord the two sides agreed, inter alia, to prohibit the use of their respective territories by any external agent planning aggression against or threatening the security of the other (Nkomati Accord, Art. 3, sec. 1). This meant that Mozambique would no longer permit ANC guerrillas to use its territory and that South Africa would expel the Resistencia Nacional Moçambicana (RENAMO— also known as the MNR—Moçambique Resistencia Nacional) and end support to it. While not part of the formal agreement, Pretoria also undertook to renew and expand economic activities in Mozambique, including limited management of the port of Maputo (the capital) and the rail system.

An end to insurgency in Mozambique has proved elusive, and the ANC has other, though far less convenient, infiltration routes to South Africa. But each side's calculations and commitments still obtain and help explain why the Nkomati Accord endures in spite of serious setbacks.

The accord was far more important to Mozambique than to South Africa. The Machel regime's very survival was at stake. RENAMO guerrillas were (and still are) operating in all ten of Mozambique's provinces, including areas near Maputo, and striking at critical transportation links and economic centers. The economy was (and still is) in danger of collapse. In contrast, while South Africa had been troubled by stepped-up ANC actions since 1982, its security was hardly threatened. Moreover, it had been quite successful in rooting out ANC networks. However, the government of P. W. Botha was on the verge of launching modest racial reforms—whose consequences could not be known—and it wanted to secure its borders against the ANC.

More important than the explicit terms of the Nkomati Accord over the longer term are the underlying premises. In spite of some skepticism in his government, Botha was gambling that South Africa could coexist and do business with a Marxist neighbor that was militarily dependent on the Soviet Union. By signing the pact, Mozambique was acknowledging that the region's black states could not survive South African enmity and that taking a chance on Pretoria's good faith and Western economic generosity was a better bet than continued conflict and greater reliance on the USSR and Cuba.

If it succeeds, the Nkomati Accord will restore the strong economic links between Mozambique and South Africa that existed before 1975, when the former was a virtual economic dependency of the latter. Between 1975 and 1981 trade between the two countries had fallen by 85 percent. In 1975 some 118,000 Mozambican workers were employed in South Africa and remitted most of their earnings in gold; by 1977 the number had been reduced to fewer than 45,000, and in 1978 South Africa withdrew its fixed-price gold remittances. The port of Maputo handled 7 million tons of mostly South African goods before 1975; in the 1980s, with a capacity of 9 million tons, it barely manages to take 1 million tons annually. South African restrictions on trade, investment, and workers' remittances cost Mozambique some $4 billion over the five years before the accord (Kalter 1984). Even with these cutbacks, workers' remittances and other fees from South Africa provided 70 percent of Mozambique's foreign currency earnings in 1983.

IMPLICATIONS OF THE NKOMATI ACCORD FOR MOZAMBIQUE AND SOUTH AFRICA

The West welcomed the Nkomati Accord, but most Africans and the socialist world were skeptical about what it meant for Mozambique. Some observers argue that Mozambique's opening to South Africa and the West represents a fundamental change in its socialist orientation and that it risks finding itself enmeshed in a made-in-South Africa security and economic net. From the "liberationist" perspective, Tanzanian President Julius Nyerere's pronouncement that "Africa must face Nkomati clearly as a retreat and not pretend it is anything else" (quoted in *Weekly Review* [Nairobi], 15 February 1985) is supported by *The Economist*'s observation that Nkomati was "little more than a gun held at President Machel's head: get rid of the ANC or else" (March 1985). We will explore these interpretations below; suffice it to point out here that when Machel added up the costs of waging a counterinsurgency war against guerrillas supplied, trained, and assisted by South Africa to the stark considerations of a wrecked economic infrastructure, a deep balance of payments crisis, and a three-year drought, his calculus clearly pointed to ending, or at least mitigating, hostile relations with Pretoria, whatever the risks.*

A pliant neighbor, for whom South Africa could be the arbiter of its political orientation and its economic lodestone, would seem to fit well with the republic's objectives in the region. But was the Nkomati Accord not simply another way to drive Machel and his comrades from power or of forcing the ruling party, the Frente de Libertação de Moçambique (FRELIMO) to bring RENAMO into the government? To answer this affirmatively would imply that Pretoria preferred confrontation, or an escalation that conceivably could bring in Cuban combat troops, when cooperation was possible. Or did South African policymakers relish the prospect of a RENAMO victory and the likely scenario of South African forces being obliged to shore up a narrowly based government fighting a FRELIMO-returned-to-the-bush, assisted by neighboring states, the Soviet Union, and Cuba? A partially de-Sovietized Machel in economic lock-step with South Africa and the West clearly looked like the better bet to Botha in the long run.

Frustrated in the past in its attempts to reach out to its black neighbors to establish a "constellation" of southern African nations (with Pretoria, the region's military and economic giant, at its center of course), South Africa is at a crossroads. As it has demonstrated over the past few years, it can prevail militarily over its black neighbors—in the short term at least—but for military confrontation it has to reckon with financial and manpower costs and the likely legacy of bitterness on both sides. Alternatively it can pursue mutually beneficial economic cooperation to try to lift its own faltering

---

*Winrich Kuehne, a German scholar, would emphasize the economic determinants and the Soviet failure to bail out Mozambique (see below). I see the security and economic aspects as interdependent.

economy out of the doldrums and relieve somewhat its military burdens and international pariahdom.

While Botha has not abandoned the strategy of confrontation and coercion, he apparently chose conciliation and cooperation in Mozambique, hoping it would catch on elsewhere in the region. Yet he continued to drag his feet on Namibia—perhaps another reason why he needed to demonstrate progress in Mozambique. It would be foolhardy to predict that Botha will keep to the policy of cooperation if his constituency's fears and habitual obduracy are heightened by domestic and regional strife and international actions against South Africa. However, at the time, as Simon Jenkins observed, "The government of P. W. Botha [was] desperate to protect Nkomati" (*The Economist*, March 1985).

RESPONSE OF THE FRONTLINE STATES*

There are many subplots and actors littering the Nkomati landscape, so it is difficult to predict that the accord will hold. But it is important that a standard for cooperation in the southern African region has been established which has implications for others besides the two protagonists. In spite of the protestations of several of the Frontline leaders—Zambia's President Kenneth Kaunda gave it only the faintest of public blessings, and Zimbabwe's Mugabe apparently shared Nyerere's chagrin—they and other neighboring states have a substantial stake in the Nkomati Accord. Malawi, Swaziland, Zambia, and Zimbabwe have traditionally utilized Mozambican rail lines and ports, and Zimbabwe is heavily dependent on the Beira-Mutare pipeline for its oil. (When it is shut down, Zimbabwe's sole source of supply is South Africa.)

Zimbabwe has been quite practical, hence cooperative, about its dependence on South Africa, its most important trading and transportation partner. Mugabe's government maintains air and land communications with South Africa, and businessmen and bankers from both countries conduct their affairs much as they did under the white-ruled regime of Ian Smith. However, in 1981 Mugabe refused to allow Zimbabwean-South African meetings at the ministerial level, and South Africa recalled twenty-four diesel locomotives from service to Zimbabwe. On other occasions, when

---

*Angola, Botswana, Mozambique, Tanzania, Zambia, and Zimbabwe.

Pretoria felt Zimbabwean rhetoric was too hostile, it slowed deliveries of oil through its ports and railroads. With such instruments of retaliation in South Africa's hands (as well as armed force), it is not surprising that Mugabe has denied permission to ANC guerrillas to operate from his country.

Some 9,000-10,000 Zimbabwean soldiers have been deployed inside Mozambique (the first 2,000 arrived in late 1982) to guard the rail and oil pipelines, as well as the oil storage depot and port facilities at Beira—all frequent RENAMO targets. Zimbabwean troops played a key role in a joint assault with Mozambican troops on a RENAMO base in the Gorongosa mountains in August 1985, and they continue to operate against RENAMO concentrations elsewhere. Zimbabwean aircraft took part in the August assault.

Malawi is in a complex and delicate situation. Since the accord, some of the heaviest fighting between FRELIMO and RENAMO has occurred near the Malawi border. Malawian authorities cannot control guerrillas operating from their territory and are loath to try for fear of worse retaliation against Malawian trade routes. If some Malawians sympathize with RENAMO, they also must live with FRELIMO, which still controls their lifelines to the sea. Machel undoubtedly pressed the point on the Malawians during a visit to Blantyre in October 1984. Malawi's (like Zimbabwe's) only alternative to Mozambican rail and port facilities is through South Africa.

Zambia is only a little better off than Malawi. It ships some of its copper through Dar es Salaam, but the Tanzania-Zambia rail line (Tazara) is overburdened, poorly run, and has insufficient rolling stock. Chronic blockages at the port of Dar es Salaam further hamper Zambian use of that route. Frequent sabotage of the Benguela railway in Angola has cut off Zambian and Zairian exports of copper and cobalt from Atlantic Ocean ports. Both countries are therefore heavily dependent on South African routes.

Kaunda has often walked the perilous path of cooperation and confrontation with South Africa. He met Prime Minister John Vorster at Victoria Falls in 1975 and P. W. Botha at the Botswana-South Africa border in April 1982, and he convened the parties to the Namibian imbroglio in Lusaka in 1984. He has frequently affirmed African acceptance of South Africa's "rightful" place on the continent, echoing the Lusaka Manifesto of 1969. But Kaunda has also provided safe haven to anti-Rhodesian and anti-South African guerrilla movements, at great peril and cost to his country. (Rhodesian forces struck camps and headquarters of the Zimbabwe

African People's Union [ZAPU] in Zambia, as well as the Tazara railway, several times during the struggle for Zimbabwean independence.) It is perhaps Kaunda's efforts to keep open communications with South Africa and his close relations with the West that have kept him off Pretoria's "enemies list"—thus far anyway. Pretoria may see Kaunda as an eventual interlocutor between it and the ANC, whose headquarters is in Lusaka.

In 1980 South Africa's black neighbors, led by the Frontline States, embarked on a highly touted effort to escape South Africa's economic embrace by establishing the Southern African Development Coordination Council (SADCC). The consortium was conceived in the full awareness that autonomy from South Africa was a distant dream at best. Such autonomy will remain even more remote if Mozambique's railroad and oil pipelines to the sea are closed to its neighbors by guerrilla actions.

Thus the Frontline States have an interest in a peaceful Mozambique. (The development of a regional transportation infrastructure through Mozambique is one of SADCC's key objectives.) And they hope to avoid being sucked more deeply into the fighting within Mozambique; Zimbabwean troops have already suffered casualties there. Most of these states do business with Pretoria, and the Nkomati Accord is different from their own policies regarding South Africa only in degree and symbolism. Swaziland has a nonaggression agreement with South Africa, and Botswana and Lesotho have pledged nonaggression but are trying to fend off formal pacts. They and the Frontline States can hardly fault Mozambique for making cooperation official.

SOVIET-MOZAMBICAN RELATIONS

It is conventionally believed that because the USSR has a relatively small stake in Mozambique—compared to its stake in Angola and Ethiopia—it is not distressed at the prospect of a loosening of ties with its formerly close ally. Indeed the Soviet Union has been remarkably restrained in the face of the Nkomati Accord. Apart from characteristic warnings about dealing with "duplicitous" South Africa and the "imperialist" United States, the Soviets apparently have placed no serious obstacles in the way of Machel's quest for a regional modus vivendi and closer economic and even military relations with the West.

MOZAMBIQUE: THE NKOMATI ACCORD   55

Mozambique's international posture has been comfortably, if at times mutedly, pro-Soviet, although Machel has repeatedly denied Soviet requests for bases on Mozambique's long Indian Ocean coast. However, it cannot have escaped the USSR's attention that its footholds in southern Africa, and its potential influence in the inevitable (to Moscow) racial conflagration in South Africa, are being challenged. For example, Mozambique's agreement to choke off the ANC's guerrilla activities is a blow to the Soviet Union, the ANC's principal non-African patron. Nevertheless, Soviet support for Mozambique has been fairly steady and has increased when the Mozambicans have asked for more. Following the signing of a treaty of friendship in 1977, the Soviets poured in advisers and materiel to help Mozambique shore up its defenses against an increasingly aggressive Rhodesia. By 1981 there were 550 Soviet and East European and 1,000 Cuban military advisers attached to the Mozambican army. East Germany virtually controlled Mozambique's security services. Moreover, a plethora of economic projects brought nearly 2,000 Soviet and East European technicians to the country (Clement 1985: 30).

When RENAMO stepped up its activities in the early 1980s, the Soviets increased their own military involvement, providing FRELIMO with MIG-21s, MI-24 helicopter gunships, advanced surface-to-air missiles, armored vehicles, tanks, artillery, and small weapons and ammunition. Soviet naval ships have visited Maputo on a number of occasions and were conspicuously present following a South African air attack on Maputo in January 1981. The Soviet ambassador to Mozambique warned at the time of military reprisals "if anyone attacks us or our friends" (Isaacman and Isaacman 1983b: 50).

In 1982, a number of high-level military exchanges took place between Mozambique and the USSR. Mozambican officials were received at the highest level in Moscow in May. In a follow-up visit to Maputo, Gen. Aleksey Yepishev, chief of the Main Political Directorate of the Soviet Army and Navy, declared that Moscow "will give every support" to Mozambican political and military needs (Clement 1985: 40). Machel had meetings with Soviet Defense Minister Dmitri Ustinov in late 1982 in Moscow (at the time of the funeral of Leonid Brezhnev), after which another Soviet military delegation visited Mozambique. Machel met privately with party leader Yuri Andropov, Foreign Minister Andrei Gromyko, and Ustinov on his way to the annual conference of nonaligned states in New Delhi in March 1983.

Apparently he received the assurances he required, for he reiterated his fealty to the socialist alliance. In May South Africa attacked an ANC camp near Maputo, and TASS, the Soviet news agency, responded as follows:

> The Soviet Union considers it necessary to declare once again its solidarity with the People's [Republic of] Mozambique, its invariable support for the Mozambican people in their indomitable struggle against the forces of imperialism, colonialism, and racism (Clement 1985: 40).

Notwithstanding its rhetorical and military support, Soviet training, tactics, and armaments have proved inadequate and at times irrelevant to the prosecution of the counterinsurgency war. Mozambicans did not hide their chagrin at the often poor quality of Soviet equipment and training. In addition, more significant strains in Mozambican-Soviet relations occurred as a result of economic differences of opinion.

Machel traveled to Moscow in late 1980 to ask for association with the Council for Mutual Economic Assistance (COMECON, the economic community of the Warsaw Pact) and an increase in economic assistance from the Soviets. The request to join COMECON was denied (the Soviets have admitted only two non-European countries to full membership, neither in Africa). Mozambique apparently decided then that modest increases in Soviet aid would not bail it out of its worsening economic crisis and that "the socialist countries were either unable to or unwilling to provide capital and advanced technology on the scale required by Mozambique to achieve its ambitious billion dollar development projects" (Isaacman and Isaacman 1983b: 53).

Had Mozambique been "winning" the guerrilla war, Machel might have held it more firmly in the socialist camp. However, the insurgency was expanding, South Africa was intervening, and the economy was seemingly beyond repair; the rejection of the bid to join COMECON seems to have tipped the balance. The Nkomati Accord followed.

As noted, the Soviet response to the Nkomati Accord has been muted. However, the Soviets commemorated the anniversary of Mozambican independence in 1984 in a national newspaper that deals with agricultural issues rather than in *Pravda*, thus showing their intense displeasure (Clement 1985: 42). Nevertheless, subsequent high-level treatment of Machel in 1984 and the continued flow of Soviet arms (additional MI-24 helicopters arrived in early 1985, and a three-year oil credit has been established, meeting 60 percent of Mozambique's needs in 1985) reflect Moscow's continuing interest in Mozambique. At the same time, its failure to influence the Machel government's move toward closer relations with the West marks the limits of Soviet influence. But as Isaacman and Isaacman put it, "In the final analysis [military] support from the socialist countries represents the only possible counter-balance to South African might" (1983a: 181).

OPENING TO THE WEST: 1982

Even while pursuing Marxism-Leninism and maintaining close relations with the USSR, Mozambique had never closed its doors to economic relations with the West. Perhaps "reopening" better describes the events of 1982. Mozambique had announced in 1978 that it was ready "to develop friendly and cooperative relations with all states, irrespective of their social systems" (FRELIMO, "Extracts from the Report of the Standing Political Committee"; cited in Isaacman and Isaacman 1983a: 185). A number of agreements followed between 1978 and 1982—for example, a $40 million loan agreement with Great Britain; a $15 million aid package with the Netherlands; a $140 million agricultural and industrial agreement with Italy; a $450 million loan from France; and a $170 million railway project with Canada, Portugal, and France. Even the U.S. Export-Import Bank loaned Mozambique funds to purchase General Electric locomotives manufactured in Brazil (Isaacman and Isaacman 1983a: 186). In 1979 South Africa and the West took about 80 percent of Mozambique's exports.

After independence Mozambique hewed to a relatively narrow definition of socialist trransformation. It limited foreign investment, collectivized agriculture, and nationalized sectors of the economy "that were considered vital to national sovereignty and the transition to a socialist economy" such as the country's only coal mine and petroleum processing facility, banks, and insurance companies (Isaacman and Isaacman 1983a: 162-63). It refused to join the Lomé Convention, the IMF and IBRD, and resisted West German insistence on the deletion of the "Berlin Clause" (which denies West German jurisdiction over West Berlin), thus foregoing assistance from that quarter. Indeed, as enunciated at the Third Party Congress in 1977, FRELIMO seemed dedicated to the notion of "class struggle" and "the destruction of capitalism" (Isaacman and Isaacman 1983a: 121).

By 1981 the Mozambican leadership apparently realized that its nascent Marxism and military and economic links to the USSR and the East were providing neither military security nor economic progress. Machel looked first to Portugal to press Mozambique's case with the West and South Africa. President Antonio Eanes's visit to Maputo in late 1981 marked the beginning of a campaign to overcome the mutual resentment and distrust of the immediate post-independence years. The former metropole had more to live down than a bloody ten-year guerrilla war. Its four hundred years of colonial rule had been marked by military conquest, violent indigenous resistance and repression, the export of slaves (some one million in the nineteenth century), and an influx of Portuguese immigrants who dominated the economy (Isaacman and Isaacman 1983a: 43).*

When all but 20,000 of the 200,000 Portuguese settlers precipitously abandoned Mozambique after independence, the new nation found itself bereft of private capital and skilled and managerial personnel (Isaacman and Isaacman 1983a: 145ff.). The ports and railway system lost 7,000 skilled and semi-skilled workers. The commercial services and transportation sectors virtually collapsed. The burden of integrating most of the ex-settlers—apart from some tens of thousands who settled in South Africa—fell on the weak Portuguese economy, further straining Portugal's still tumultuous post-coup political situation. The Portuguese hope, even now, to see at least some of these *retornados* go back to Mozambique; their return would bring a prospect of reestablishing commercial links between the two countries.

Notwithstanding frequent well-publicized missions to Mozambique—including Prime Minister Pinto Balsamao's state visit in June 1982, Prime Minister Mario Soares in 1984, and a second call by Eanes in April 1985—Portuguese investment, credits, and assistance to Mozambique have been modest. Moreover, few retornados have found their way back thus far.

It is unlikely that Machel expected Portugal to become a large investor or aid donor. But by dangling commercial opportunities and allowing Portuguese ex-settlers to return, he was preparing the

---

*Immigration reached 10,000 per year in 1959.

ground for Western businessmen in general to reenter Mozambique—and hoping to see diplomats close behind. Lisbon was to serve as the political middleman. Mozambique placed orders for $40 million worth of Portuguese goods at an international trade fair in Maputo in 1982 (Washington 1982) and in April accepted a Portuguese offer of military assistance. The pact was more symbolic than substantive. Yet it marked a new era of improved relations and set the stage for Portugal to press its European and U.S. allies to reenter Mozambique.

THE U.S. ROLE

U.S.-Mozambican relations had been on a mini roller coaster since independence. The newly installed Mozambican government, partly out of revolutionary zeal, partly out of anger over NATO's support of Portugal during the wars of liberation in both Angola and Mozambique, kept its distance from the United States and the West in general. In turn, the U.S. Congress banned direct aid to Mozambique in 1977, allowing only food assistance under Public Law 480. However, the Carter administration's Rhodesian policies helped mitigate Mozambican suspicions of the United States. At a meeting with President Jimmy Carter in New York in 1978, Machel offered to "wipe the slate clean" (Isaacman and Isaacman 1983a: 185). Relations nose-dived again in 1981, when Mozambique expelled four U.S. Embassy personnel in Maputo, allegedly for spying for the CIA and having provided intelligence to South Africa for a raid on ANC facilities in January. The new administration under Ronald Reagan failed to name a new ambassador to replace its departing one and suspended food shipments.

The U.S. government received a number of indications in 1982—from Mozambican interlocutors, private businessmen, and Portugal—that the Machel government would be interested in improving relations and hoped the United States would help ease tensions between Mozambique and South Africa. The United States finally accepted the offer to end the freeze in U.S.-Mozambican relations when the Namibian-Angolan side of its regional policy of "constructive engagement" was at an impasse. Not only had Washington failed to bring Namibia nearer to independence and to get the Cubans out of Angola, but also the Western Contact Group was fraying. Improved relations with Mozambique would provide an opportunity to ameliorate the conflict between South Africa and at least one of its neighbors. (The United States had already exhorted Pretoria not to upset the still fragile Zimbabwean government, upon which Washington had lavished considerable aid and confidence.) Deputy Secretary of State Frank Wisner visited Maputo in December 1982 in response to the Mozambican feelers. Assistant Secretary Chester Crocker followed in January 1983, combining his visit with consultations in Pretoria, presumably to test South Africa's interests in a modus vivendi with Machel.

While Crocker and his aides have not claimed credit for the success of the talks or the Nkomati Accord, it was no secret that the United States had helped bring Mozambique and South Africa together. One Crocker aide has described the U.S. role as that of "midwife" of the Nkomati Accord. The U.S. government intensified its support for the accord and sought economic support from its allies to sweeten the package for the Machel government. U.S. businessmen have visited Mozambique on a number of occasions, and U.S. aid to Mozambique has increased considerably since the accord—particularly food aid (210,000 tons over 1984-85). In 1985 the State Department proposed $1.1 million for nonlethal military assistance but was blocked by Congress. Nevertheless, economic assistance was launched in late 1984 (the first since 1977) and raised to $15 million in 1985. Including a growing food emergency relief program, U.S. aid to Mozambique surpassed $60 million in 1985.

MOZAMBIQUE'S ROAD TO THE NKOMATI ACCORD

The Nkomati Accord reflected Mozambique's hope that peace with Pretoria would remove the prop holding up the RENAMO guerrilla movement opposing it. However, events since March 1984 indicate clearly that the roots of Mozambique's problems are internal as well as external, and that if it is to cope successfully with the security threat, it will have to overcome its economic crisis as well. Below we analyze both the opposition movement and the economic situation.

EXTERNAL FACTORS: RENAMO

How could RENAMO, a ragtag amalgam of racial and ethnic groups and diverse sponsors, without a program or clear ideology, threaten the Machel government?* And why cannot FRELIMO's 25,000-man army (which outguns the 10,000 or so guerrillas) restore a modicum of tranquility?

Formed in 1976 by Rhodesian security officials with some help from South African intelligence officers, RENAMO filled its ranks with Portuguese ex-settlers and black and white members of the colonial police and army who had fled Mozambique after independence. Over time FRELIMO defectors and Rhodesian-recruited mercenaries joined the movement. Its bases were primarily in Maina and Sofala provinces. In what is considered the first phase of its activities, RENAMO forces operated inside Mozambique during the Rhodesian civil war, first as intelligence gatherers, later conducting hit-and-run attacks on Mugabe's guerrilla bases near the border, and eventually against Mozambican transport, communications, and economic targets. By 1979 "Rhodesia was regularly resupplying by air [RENAMO] guerrilla military bases in the mountains along the Mozambican-Rhodesian border and the Gorongosa mountains further inland" (Isaacman and Isaacman 1982: 5).

As Rhodesia approached independence, RENAMO was on the run. In late 1979 FRELIMO overran the main RENAMO base in the Gorongosa mountains, killing one of its two black leaders, Andre Matzangaiza. It was reported that "many soldiers and leaders were killed" (Isaacman and Isaacman 1982: 5), but most of the guerrillas escaped. In June 1980 Mozambican troops destroyed another base, inflicting heavy casualties. By then South Africa had picked up the remnants and began retraining and supplying cadre at bases in the Transvaal. Pretoria moved RENAMO's radio transmitter, Voz da Africa Livre, from Rhodesia, and broadcasts resumed in 1980.

Led by its founder, Orlando Cristina, a shadowy Portuguese with connections to the Portuguese secret police and a prominent Portuguese businessman who hoped to regain his former holdings in Mozambique, RENAMO soon reentered Mozambique in force and established bases in the central provinces near the Zimbabwe border. The second phase of its insurgency had begun—this time fully backed by South Africa and serving its interests. (Ironically, attacks on the Cahora Bassa power line to South Africa in 1981 resulted in power shortages in the Transvaal.) In October guerrillas,

---

*RENAMO claims to be "anti-Communist," but it is doubtful that anti-communism is its moving force or even a comprehensible concept for most of its guerrillas. Of course anti-communism sells in South Africa and among right-wing sympathizers in the West.

probably accompanied by South African "instructors," sabotaged road and rail bridges linking Beira and Mutari. By late 1981 RENAMO had moved back into Maina and Sofala provinces and established a base in Inhambane province (*Africa Confidential* 23, 15 [21 July 1982]).

By 1982 RENAMO was operating in seven of Mozambique's provinces, albeit mostly in lightly populated areas. By the middle of the year, only the main towns in several provinces were safe, and twelve foreign technicians had been killed. Machel postponed a visit to West Europe in July (*Africa Confidential* 23, 15 [21 July 1982]) —apparently because of scheduling difficulties, but observers were quick to ascribe the postponement to the escalating RENAMO threat.

If the postponement reflected Machel's concern about the deteriorating security situation, South Africa, too, was reexamining its options. While earlier only a few officials had believed that RENAMO represented a serious alternative to FRELIMO, the possibility that the Machel regime could be toppled came to the fore in the South African State Security Council in mid-1982 (*Africa Confidential* 23, 15 [21 July 1982]). But there was as much concern about a RENAMO victory as there was a desire for it: would FRELIMO not return to the bush to press the guerrilla war and leave Pretoria with the unwelcome task of defending a loosely knit and disputatious government? The South Africans also had to consider whether Machel would call for Cuban combat troops were he on the verge of defeat.

In April 1983, Cristina was murdered at his farm in South Africa, probably by rivals in RENAMO, producing confusion and exciting fissiparous tendencies long evident in the movement. There had already been at least one power struggle, following the June 1980 destruction of a RENAMO base. Indeed, as indicated, it is questionable whether RENAMO was ever a unified organization, and elements operating in the north, in Tete and Cabo Delgado provinces, may have been at best semi-autonomous bands of guerrillas and freebooters (*Africa Confidential* 23, 3 [30 January 1985]).

By 1984 RENAMO seems to have reorganized sufficiently— this time with military leaders such as Alfonso Dhaklama (sometimes called "Jacama") more fully sharing the political leadership—to operate on the outskirts of Maputo, cutting roads and rail lines, preventing the distribution of emergency drought relief, and continuing acts of terrorism against civilians, including foreign nationals.

RENAMO stepped up its activities following the signing of the Nkomati Accord, probably with a view to demonstrating that it was still a force, with or without South African help (although Pretoria had made a last, large supply effort prior to the accord).

Until mid-1985 most observers believed that South African assistance to RENAMO had been reduced to a trickle at best. Maputo consistently charged Pretoria with bad faith, but apart from alleged sightings of South African air and sea drops and a few skirmishes with guerrillas near the South African border, Mozambique produced no firm evidence. However, Zimbabwean troops captured RENAMO headquarters in the Gorongosa mountains in August 1985, and they turned up substantial evidence of continued South African contact with and support of RENAMO. Deputy Foreign Minister Louis Nel had visited RENAMO headquarters several times since the accord, and it appears that the South Africans had built an airfield to facilitate the visits and supply efforts.

Who ordered that the RENAMO-South Africa connection be maintained—and why—remains uncertain. It may be presumed that some South African officials wanted to keep pressure on Machel, hoping to force him to negotiate with RENAMO; others may have felt that the Nkomati Accord had deprived them of a military victory. At a minimum, South Africa undoubtedly did not want to be judged as abandoning RENAMO and felt that if RENAMO was to be kept alive, it ought also to be kept under South African influence.

The South Africans soon learned that their influence on RENAMO had limits, however. At a meeting in Pretoria in October 1984, Foreign Minister Pik Botha, flanked by Mozambique's principal negotiator, Jacinto Veloso, and RENAMO's European-based political spokesman, Evo Fernandes, announced that FRELIMO and RENAMO would seek reconciliation. Machel would remain president, hostilities would cease, and South Africa would chair a joint commission to implement an agreement. The next day, Botha announced a "cease-fire"—which both sides immediately renounced. After demanding that RENAMO be given the premiership if Machel remained as president, Fernandes suddenly departed for Lisbon (under orders from his Portuguese patron, according to *Africa Confidential* 23, 3 [30 January 1985]).

Further evidence of South Africa's loose control of RENAMO came in January 1985, when President Botha admitted publicly that "elements" inside South Africa were still helping it. Whether Botha had been ignorant of the connections or unable to do anything about them, his personal prestige suffered. The revelation of continuing support for RENAMO undermined not only South Africa's commitments to the Nkomati Accord, but also its ability to press similar accords on its other black neighbors, including Angola. In an effort to regain good faith, Botha ordered the Chief of the Defense Staff, Constand Viljoen, to end all aid to RENAMO and threatened to court martial anyone who disobeyed (*The Economist*, March 1985). Botha also sent his foreign minister to Malawi, Somalia, and the Comoros in January to seek an end to the transit of supplies to RENAMO from these states.

RENAMO has thus demonstrated its ability to spoil but not to wreck the Nkomati Accord. So long as it continues to receive support from anti-Communist sympathizers in Portugal, Brazil, the United States, West Germany, Morocco, Saudi Arabia, and Zaire (*The Economist*, March 1985), it can survive without great South African support. But it is still far from overthrowing the Machel regime, and reconciliation with FRELIMO also seems remote.

Given South Africa's own economic problems, Mozambique's suspicion of its intentions, and its own chronic security crisis, little of South Africa's promised aid and investment has flowed to Mozambique. Moreover, Machel has yet to take up Pretoria's offer to provide security forces to guard the Cahora Bassa hydroelectric power lines, which are as important to South Africa (which takes 80 percent of the output) as to Mozambique.

INTERNAL FACTORS: ECONOMIC CRISIS

If the Nkomati Accord has not brought Mozambique much relief from its security problems, are its economic prospects any better than they were in 1982, when it initiated the opening to the West? The security and economic problems are related. Just as the insurgency impedes commerce, transportation, and development, so the poor state of the economy renders the guerrillas' job the easier. Where FRELIMO's statist economic policies have been tried—and mostly failed—Mozambicans are hostile to the central government. Where Maputo's fiat does not run and basic social and administrative services are not available, the population has little loyalty to the government and is ripe for the insurgents' arguments that FRELIMO does not care for the people.

Economic mismanagement, irrelevant organizational prescriptions (for example, setting up state and cooperative farms as opposed to promoting smallholder agriculture), and a vicious three-year drought (1980-83) have probably done more to loosen Machel's hold on the population than RENAMO has. Yet clearly not all Mozambique's economic problems can be laid at Machel's door. Amidst a plethora of gloomy statistics is the historical fact that Mozambique's pre-1975 modern economy, based on Portuguese settler enterprise, skills, and capital and on cheap African unskilled labor, was hardly self-sustaining. In spite of the South African connection, the gross national product had fallen 17 percent between 1970 and 1975 in the throes of the civil war. The overall balance of payments was negative throughout the 1970s (apart from 1975 and 1976, when there was a sudden influx of foreign aid). By 1976 the economy began its most serious decline following the departure of most of the Portuguese. Sugar, cashew, and cement production fell by nearly half. When the government decided to enforce UN sanctions against Rhodesia in 1976—for which it was applauded in the West—it lost annually between $105 and $165 million in port fees, freight charges, and remittances of Mozambican workers. Support for Rhodesian guerrillas operating from Mozambique and for over 100,000 Rhodesian refugees cost another $100-150 million annually (Isaacman and Isaacman 1983a: 145-48). As noted, the decline in economic relations with South Africa ended up costing some $4 billion.

Notwithstanding these daunting figures, Mozambique launched a costly program of socialist development for which it was ill-structured and underfinanced. Admittedly only the government could pick up the pieces from the departing Portuguese, given the dearth of indigenous capital, entrepreneurship, and skills. But the guidelines recommended to the Third Party Congress by the FRELIMO Central Committee in February 1977 compounded the government's burden:

> The communal villages are the fundamental lever for liberating the people in the rural areas. Industry is the dynamizing factor for economic development. The construction of heavy industry constitutes the decisive factor for our total independence. . . . The building of socialism demands that the economy be centrally planned and directed by the State (quoted in Isaacman and Isaacman 1983a: 148).

By 1983, after five years of costly involvement in the Rhodesian war, its own spreading civil war, the severe drought, and a faltering world economy, Mozambique's trade deficit stood at $500 million and its external debt to non-Communist countries at $1.4 billion;

the current accounts deficit was $300 million (U. S. Department of Commerce 1984). Mozambique would seem to have had no alternative but to reorient its domestic and international policies.

FRELIMO's Fourth Party Congress spoke of reforms that must precede further socialist development and prescribed (among other things) greater reliance on smallholder, family-run agriculture. Vague pronouncements about foreign investment did not greatly alter policies, and there were plenty of reassurances about devotion to socialism and nonalignment. However, shortly after the Fourth Party Congress, extensive personnel shakeups in economic ministries seemed to betoken a real shift to more pragmatic policies. In 1984 the Bank of Mozambique issued "Economic Action Program for 1984-86," a document that gave substance to the earlier signals of change. It prescribed (inter alia) increased support and resources to family and private farms; an import substitution program; rehabilitation of ports and railways to neighboring countries; rehabilitation of tourism (a South African interest); and encouragement of foreign investment; in addition, it hinted broadly at currency devaluation and other price, tax, and credit measures.

By the end of 1984 Mozambique finally joined the Lomé Convention, signed a modified Berlin Clause, and began negotiations with the IBRD and IMF. It joined both organizations, and by mid-1985 the IBRD had provided $45 million in aid and the IMF was negotiating a loan and technical assistance. American investors and bankers made a number of visits to Mozambique and were warmly received—among them a team led by former Defense Secretary Melvin Laird, and David Rockefeller of City Bank of New York. American business activity seems likely to develop; oil exploration agreements have been signed with Exxon, Shell, Amoco, and other oil companies, as well as with several Japanese and European firms.

If the domestic reforms and foreign investment are realized, Mozambique will have moved far from the visions of the Third Party Congress. While such a move hardly constitutes an abandonment of socialism or a willful placing of Mozambique's economic fate in the hands of the West, Machel has taken great risks in his opening to the West and signing of the Nkomati Accord. Perhaps Machel has a hidden agenda or has assured his antagonists that he does, and once Mozambique's security is assured and the economy revived—by means of a program modeled on the 1920s Soviet New Economic Policy—Mozambique will spring back into the struggle to build socialism at home and help liberate South Africa from white minority rule. However, such an agenda is unlikely because whatever Machel's intentions, Mozambique's economic reconstruction will take decades, not years, and can take place only with sustained and far-reaching Western investment and aid. If such a scenario came to pass, would Mozambique then be ready to gamble its recovery away in domestic economic and regional military adventurism?

CONCLUSIONS

There are many contingencies in attempting to chart a course for Mozambique after the Nkomati Accord. Many, such as world economic conditions, are beyond the control of the protagonists. Internal stresses in Mozambique and South Africa could also alter the regional dynamics which made the accord possible. However, Mozambique's desperate security and economic problems are unlikely to change, so it is likely to pursue the accord to its logical conclusion. That means substantial South African influence in Mozambique and a greater Western role in its economy.

Machel undoubtedly entered into the Nkomati Accord fully aware that Mozambique could be "hooked" by South Africa and the West. Yet he may also believe that he has hooked the fishermen: South Africa and the United States have a major stake in the accord and will probably be willing to give Machel considerable leeway in order to keep him from reneging on it. However, if future investment and aid are linked to an even more radical tilt to the West by Mozambique, its government will almost certainly resist. Mozambique has not abandoned its socialist objectives nor its friendly relations with the East, even though it is willing to make tradeoffs on both. For example, Mozambique's recent UN voting record is far less hostile to the United States than it had been, but it has made it so by abstentions and absences on votes that the United States considers important rather than by taking a pro-U.S. position. At the same time, Mozambique is one of the few countries to have established relations with Afghanistan since the Soviet invasion.

It would be a mistake, then, to count Mozambique among the formerly "radical" states that have begun a return to the Western fold, just as it was a mistake to write off many of them in the 1970s. It would be more instructive to recognize that African states are more flexible and realistic than their professions of socialist or other doctrines would suggest. What does not work will be discarded, given reasonable alternatives. Thus Mozambique is currently exploring its options. If the Nkomati Accord is accompanied by a great deal of unacceptable ideology, Mozambique will turn away from it. Mozambique is not "back" in the Western camp just as it never was an obedient client of the Soviet Union.

Another lesson of the Nkomati Accord for the West is that South Africa alone cannot deliver the economic or security guarantees that Mozambique requires. Indeed given South Africa's current economic problems, it should not be expected to do so. Nor is it in U.S. and Western interests to be judged in partnership with Pretoria. Thus Western economic institutions—multinational corporations and lending agencies—will have to carry the external burden of Mozambique's recovery. They may do so for essentially economic reasons, but their actions will have regional political implications.

Mozambique's possibly last-gasp attempt to balance its international relations and pursue more moderate economic and political policies depends on the Western response as well as on South Africa's military restraint. While political-military efforts may kill some of the weeds of the RENAMO insurgency, economic development could more effectively choke them off.

CONCLUSION: COMING TO TERMS WITH RADICAL SOCIALISM

Michael Clough

The Soviet Union's African "victories" of the mid-1970s have had significant and somewhat contradictory effects on U.S. policy toward Africa and the world. The Angolan debacle of 1975 seriously eroded public support for "detente" with the Soviet Union, but it also caused the Ford administration to adopt a much more regionally sensitive policy toward Africa, especially the continent's explosive southern cone. In a landmark speech in April 1976 in Lusaka, Zambia, Secretary of State Henry Kissinger (1) Signaled the beginning of active U.S. involvement in efforts to negotiate settlements that would end armed conflict and achieve the internationally recognized independence of Rhodesia (Zimbabwe) and Namibia, and (2) Made it clear that there were limits on the extent to which any government of the United States could positively associate with a South Africa organized on the principle of apartheid. From the Lusaka speech through 1985, U.S. policymakers pursued an approach in Africa that was, with some exceptions, essentially regionalist (Kitchen and Clough 1984 and Clough 1985-86).

Reacting to events in the Horn of Africa, in early 1978 the Carter administration briefly adopted a "tougher," more globalist posture toward African conflicts (Vance 1983: 84-92; Oudes and Clough 1978-79: 86-87). This change accounted for the marked difference between the administration's low-key, measured response to a rebel invasion of Zaire's Shaba province in March 1977 and President Carter's strong reaction to a similar invasion in May 1978 (Price 1978: 51-58; Garthoff 1985: 623-30; Mangold 1979). Regionalists within the administration regained the upper hand quickly as far as most African issues were concerned. However, their efforts to convince President Carter to recognize the MPLA government in Angola suffered a serious setback. The public reaction to Soviet intervention in the Horn largely finished off detente. More generally, the "pattern" of developments beginning with Angola and Ethiopia, including the fall of the Shah in Iran and President Anastasio Somoza in Nicaragua, and culminating in the Soviet invasion of Afghanistan in 1980 provided the impetus for a more conservative, hawkish public mood typified by the rhetoric of Ronald Reagan and his supporters in the 1980 presidential election.

The Reagan administration seemed certain to adopt a conservative globalist approach to African issues. For a complex mix of reasons, it did not (Clough 1985-86: 4-7). Instead Assistant Secretary of State Chester Crocker won the support of President Reagan and Secretary of State Alexander Haig for an African strategy that, although conservative in disposition, was still more regionalist than globalist. In 1985, however, a somewhat disparate group of politicians, officials, and opinion leaders coalesced in support of a more aggressive, ideological, and interventionist posture toward radical socialist regimes in the Third World. This development has led to pressure for direct assistance to Jonas Savimbi and UNITA in Angola and has greatly complicated the Reagan administration's efforts to aid the Machel government in Mozambique. The implications for Ethiopia and other radical socialist governments in Africa are not yet clear.

Ironically, this new wave of globalism is cresting just as it is becoming clear that the Soviet Union's African gains of the mid-1970s have proven to be illusory and ephemeral. The dire predictions of conservative globalists quoted in the introduction have not materialized. As the essays in this volume evidence, the Soviet Union's successes in Angola, Ethiopia, and Mozambique do not look as impressive (or ominous) in 1985 as they did in 1977-78. In fact, most analysts now agree that Soviet prestige and influence in Africa declined steadily from 1978 through 1984, just as most skeptical regionalists predicted it would. U.S. influence, in contrast, rose substantially during this period.

There is thus a disjuncture between popular images of a growing Soviet threat in Africa and the reality of declining Soviet influence. Unfortunately, it appears that images rather than reality are beginning to drive American policy. Before embarking on a quixotic crusade to "roll back" Soviet influence and promote the spread of "freedom," U.S. officials should take a closer look at the U.S.-Soviet balance sheet on the continent for the period 1975-84. They should also examine deeply and dispassionately the factors underlying the Soviet Union's changing fortunes in Africa. We present such an analysis below.

U.S.-SOVIET BALANCE SHEET IN AFRICA, 1975-84

Soviet successes in Angola and Ethiopia in the mid-1970s did not create the "bandwagon" effect that many conservative globalists expected.* Since 1977 the Soviet Union has not gained a single important new ally on the continent. To the contrary, Soviet influence in a number of African countries—including Guinea, Algeria, Guinea-Bissau, Madagascar, Mozambique, Benin, and the Congo—has declined, in some cases markedly. Western influence, in contrast, has increased in all of these countries. In addition, Moscow suffered a serious setback in Zimbabwe in 1980, when a radical socialist, Robert Mugabe, won an overwhelming election victory (following an agreement brokered by Great Britain) and chose to rely primarily on Western economic and military assistance. Finally, the limits of Soviet influence have been highlighted by the USSR's inability to consolidate its position in Angola and Ethiopia. Let us examine these developments in greater detail.

One of the greatest concerns of conservative globalists was that success of Soviet intervention in Angola and Ethiopia would cause leaders in other African countries to throw in their lot with the Soviet Union. Having witnessed the Soviet Union's willingness to act decisively on behalf of its allies and the corresponding U.S. unwillingness and/or inability to do so, African leaders would (it was feared) choose to go with the seemingly stronger and more reliable of the two superpowers. For example, Bruce Porter argued that "Soviet-backed military victories have contributed to a growing perception among third world leaders that the future lies with the East rather than the West and that it is, in any event, imprudent not to maintain a good relationship with Moscow" (1984: 239). Stephen David portentously concluded that "It is hard to avoid the central political lesson that has emerged: alignment with the Soviet Union proved demonstrably superior to alignment with the United States" (1979: 70). On the basis of similar logic, Thomas Henriksen concluded that Soviet prospects in Africa were "bright" (1983: 271).

By almost any measure, however, the number of African states aligned with the Soviet Union has declined steadily since reaching a high point in 1977-78. One measure is treaty agreements and abrogations. During the 1970s the Soviet Union entered into treaty relationships with five African countries: Egypt (May 1971), Somalia

*On "bandwagonning," see Walt (1975).

(July 1974), Angola (October 1976), Mozambique (March 1977), and Ethiopia (November 1978) (Iman 1983). Since 1978 only one additional African country—the Congo—has signed a treaty of friendship and cooperation with Moscow, and that treaty did not contain a military clause (see *Africa Contemporary Record* 1982-83: B380). Egypt and Somalia abrogated their treaties with the Soviets in 1976 and 1977 respectively and are now counted among Moscow's strongest foes on the continent. Moreover, the Machel government's decision to seek military assistance from the West and sign a nonaggression pact in March 1984 with South Africa (the Nkomati Accord) have rendered its treaty with Moscow relatively meaningless.

Military assistance trends provide a second indicator that the Soviet gains of the mid-1970s have not caused a significant shift in the strategic orientation of most African states. Between 1976 and 1980 roughly one third of Africa's fifty independent states received the bulk of their military supplies from the Soviet Union and its allies.* In percentage terms this constituted a small increase over preceding periods. Most of the increase was accounted for by the emergence of radical socialist governments in the five Portuguese-speaking territories that gained their independence in 1974-75. Since 1980 the number of African states dependent primarily on the Soviet Union for military support has declined; in addition, the number of arms transfer agreements between the Soviet Union and African states as a percentage of total agreements signed by African states has also declined slightly (Grimmett 1984: 21). Angola, the Congo, Ethiopia, Mozambique, Tanzania, Algeria, and Libya have signed major arms agreements with Moscow in the 1980s. Tanzania's arms purchases from the Soviets have never led to close military links between the two countries. Moreover, Tanzania's appetite for arms decreased greatly in the early 1980s, following the end of its intervention in Uganda. Since 1982 the Congo, Mozambique, and Algeria have turned to the West for military assistance. As of 1985 only Angola, Ethiopia, and (in a very different respect) Libya could be counted as significant military dependencies of the Soviet Union.

---

*It is difficult to obtain detailed country-by-country data on Soviet arms transfers. The data cited in this paragraph are taken from *Foreign Military Sales and Military Assistance Facts*, published annually by the U.S. Department of Defense. Information on specific arms agreements can be found in *African Defense Journal* and *Defense and Foreign Affairs*.

CONCLUSION: COMING TO TERMS WITH RADICAL SOCIALISM 73

In 1986 forty-one African countries—more than ever before—will receive military training assistance from the United States (Security Assistance Programs, Congressional Presentation, FY 1986). Included on the list of countries that the Reagan administration proposed to aid were Algeria, Benin, the Congo, Madagascar, and all of the former Portuguese territories except Angola.* A decade earlier, most conservative globalists would have considered all of the radical socialist regimes in these countries to be firmly in the Soviet camp.

Another frequently used (and usually misused) indicator of alignment is voting behavior in the United Nations (Clough 1985). An examination of how African countries have voted on three issues of major concern to the Soviet Union—Afghanistan, Kampuchea, and illegal use of chemical and biological weapons—clearly demonstrates the limits of Soviet influence on the continent. No more than nine African countries have ever voted with the Soviet Union on *any* of these issues (in 1980), while at least twenty-three have voted against the Soviets on *all* three issues in each of the past five years. The number voting with the Soviets on any of these issues declined to only six in 1984. In that year only Libya voted with the Soviet Union on all three issues.

In short, the Soviet interventions in Angola and Ethiopia have not caused African leaders to rush to Moscow for support. By 1985 the Soviet Union had fewer reliable allies in Africa than at any time since the end of the colonial period.

A major symbolic watershed in Soviet relations with Africa occurred in April 1980, when the Zimbabwe African National Union (ZANU), led by Mugabe, won an overwhelming victory in Zimbabwe's first independent election.† A radical socialist government coming to power through elections, following negotiations brokered by a conservative British government and resulting in the so-called Lancaster House settlement, represented a sharp contrast to the transitions to independence that had occurred in Angola and Mozambique. Moreover, the compromise settlement was made possible by the Machel government—ostensibly a close ally of Moscow at the time—adding to the ideologically anomalous quality of events in Zimbabwe.** For the Soviets, however, what mattered

―――――――――
*A proposed package of military training and nonlethal supplies for Mozambique was blocked by Congress in July 1985.

†On the 1980 election and its significance, see Clough (1980) and Gregory (1981).

**On Machel's role in the Lancaster House settlements, see Davidow (1984: 89).

most was that Mugabe pointedly declined to invite East Germany, Poland, Hungary, or Czechoslovakia to participate in Zimbabwe's April 1980 independence celebrations, and reportedly cold-shouldered an attempt by Moscow to trade Foreign Minister Andrei Gromyko's presence for an agreement to issue a joint communique cementing Soviet-Zimbabwean ties. The USSR was represented instead by a low-level Politburo member, and Zimbabwe delayed until February 1981 before allowing Moscow to open an embassy in Harare. In contrast, Mugabe made a triumphant visit to Washington in August 1980 (*New York Times,* 21, 25, 27, 28 August 1980). Of more consequence substantively were Mugabe's decisions to turn over the task of integrating and training the Zimbabwean military to the British, rely on Western support for protection against pressure from South Africa, and chart a moderate economic course.*

Why did Mugabe decide to snub the Soviet Union and tilt westward (Somerville 1984; Clement 1985: 45)? Most analysts point to Moscow's consistent preference for Joshua Nkomo and the Zimbabwe African People's Union (ZAPU), ZANU's historic rival within the nationalist movement, during the liberation struggle. In this view, Mugabe's postindependence posture was motivated by bitterness over the Soviet Union's failure to aid ZANU in the past and suspicion that the Kremlin might still harbor hopes of seeing Nkomo emerge on top in an independent Zimbabwe. These were undoubtedly factors, but they were not the only or even the most important determinants of Mugabe's decision to rely so heavily on London and Washington.

Given the economic and regional security problems facing the Zimbabwe government at independence and favorable experiences with the Thatcher and Carter administrations during the transition period, Mugabe had good reason to conclude that close ties with the West would pay high dividends. Moscow lacked the economic wherewithal of Great Britain and the United States. Just as important, in 1980 a close relationship with London and Washington seemed a better way to deter South African intervention than did Soviet arms. These factors would not have been sufficient had the Mugabe government not also believed it could trust the West. Here the Carter

---

*North Korea was asked to train one new army brigade. However, that brigade performed poorly when it was used to suppress antigovernment dissidents in Matabeleland. The Zimbabwe government proceeded to phase out the North Korean advisers, turning over responsibility for retraining the brigade's officers to the British. On Zimbabwe since independence, see Clough (1983) and "Zimbabwe: A Survey"; *Economist,* 21 April 1984.

CONCLUSION: COMING TO TERMS WITH RADICAL SOCIALISM

administration's steadfast refusal to support the short-lived internal settlement—which excluded Mugabe and his supporteres—and the Thatcher government's impartial performance during and after the 1980 elections had to weigh strongly and positively in Mugabe's calculations. If the West had lacked either the resources or willingness to support his government, Mugabe would have had little choice but to cut a deal with the Kremlin.

The argument that the historic differences between ZANU and the Soviet Union prevented the Mugabe government from aligning with the East also overlooks the critical role played in Zimbabwean developments by Machel and FRELIMO. If Mugabe had desired a rapprochement with Moscow, Machel undoubtedly could have served as a go-between. Instead, based on his own government's experiences, Machel appears to have encouraged Mugabe to seek moderation and turn West.

If the above analysis is correct, the setback the Soviets suffered in Zimbabwe was far more fundamental and far-reaching than is implied by arguments that focus solely on historical antagonisms between ZANU and Moscow. That setback evidenced a structural weakness in the Soviet position in Africa; the weakness can be eased marginally but not eliminated by better intelligence and tactical decision-making by Soviet leaders.

Developments in Angola, Ethiopia, and Mozambique since 1978 have provided further evidence of the limited and fragile nature of Soviet influence in Africa. As Marcum, Henze, and Lowenkopf demonstrate in this volume, the Soviet Union has failed to consolidate its position in any of these countries. Their assessment is widely shared by other Africa watchers. For example, in February 1984 Hugo Sada, a noted French expert on African security matters, wrote as follows:

> In the three African countries in which the USSR has made strategic investments in recent years, investments serving as a base and reference point for its influence and reputation throughout the continent, Moscow is now on the defensive. What is worse, while it built its African credibility on its ability to protect allied regimes politically and militarily, it is no longer even able to face the increasingly serious security problems confronting its allies. The image of the USSR, the "military protector," is beginning to blur in Africa (1984: 29).

The limits of Soviet influence in Angola, Ethiopia, and Mozambique have been manifested in four ways. First, as Sada noted, despite Soviet support, the security situation in all three of these countries has deteriorated. In the first half of the 1980s the regimes in Luanda, Addis Ababa, and Maputo faced mounting insurgencies. Only in Ethiopia's Ogaden province has Soviet and Cuban support quelled guerrilla activity. Moreover, in both Angola and Mozambique Soviet support failed to deter South African military incursions.

Second, the Soviets have been unable to erode Western economic influence in these countries. To the contrary, all three are now more dependent on Western aid and/or trade than they were in the mid-1970s. Significantly, both Angola and Mozambique now rely on American firms for advice on managing their economic policies. By rejecting Mozambique's application for membership in late 1981, COMECON signaled to radical socialist leaders that there is no economic alternative to integration into the Western capitalist international system (Kuhne 1985). Some Western analysts maintain that this economic reality will not necessarily affect the political orientation of Third World states. Most Soviet analysts, however, reach a different conclusion. For example, Karen Brutents, an influential official in the international department of the Central Committee of the Communist Party of the USSR, issued the following warning in the late 1970s:

> The activity of revolutionary governments and progressive forces is hemmed in by their countries' continued economic dependence on imperialism and the world capitalist economy, a dependence which cannot be ended in one fell swoop, and which has serious adverse consequences for progressive orientation—both economic and political (1979: 103).

A leading American economist, Richard Feinberg, put this point more bluntly: "Moscow's inability to incorporate self-proclaimed Marxist regimes such as Angola, Mozambique, and Ethiopia into a socialist economic system will inevitably weaken Moscow's ability to dictate their foreign policies" (1983: 139).

Third, close ties with the Soviet Union have failed to prevent Angolan, Mozambican, and (to a lesser extent) Ethiopian leaders from cooperating diplomatically with the West. In the late 1970s Angolan President Agostinho Neto intervened on at least one occasion to advance Western efforts to achieve a negotiated settlement in Namibia.* Since 1982 his successor, President José Eduardo dos Santos, has engaged in intensive negotiations with the Reagan

---

*An excellent account of Neto's diplomatic contacts with the West is provided in Saunders (1983).

CONCLUSION: COMING TO TERMS WITH RADICAL SOCIALISM

administration which, were they to succeed, would produce a major American diplomatic victory, reduce the Cuban presence in Angola, and significantly decrease Angolan dependence on Moscow (Clement 1985: 31-39; Clough 1985-86). As discussed above, President Machel of Mozambique was instrumental in the Lancaster House settlement of 1979, and (as Lowenkopf documented) a Mozambican-initiated rapprochement with the United States made possible the Nkomati Accord of 1984. Moreover, Machel helped the United States broker the Lusaka Accord of February 1984 between Angola and South Africa.* In these ways, Angola and Mozambique have been consistent and reliable supporters of Western diplomatic efforts in southern Africa. In 1983 Ethiopia, while not engaging in any direct collaboration with the United States, played a crucial role in ending disputes within the Organization of African Unity over Chad and the Western Sahara in a manner that favored pro-Western forces (*African Research Bulletin,* 1-30 June 1983: 6857).

Finally, the Soviet Union has failed to decisively influence internal political developments in Ethiopia, Angola, and Mozambique. In Ethiopia (as Henze and others have documented) President Mengistu Haile Mariam has consistently resisted Soviet pressure to establish an independent, Marxist-Leninist party. In Angola and Mozambique power has remained firmly in the hands of pragmatic nationalists rather than more pro-Soviet Marxist ideologues. To date, there is no evidence that the Soviet Union will be significantly more successful in institutionalizing its influence in these three countries than it was in Algeria, Egypt, Guinea, Ghana, and Mali in the 1960s or in Somalia in the 1970s.† Thus by almost any measure, between 1978 and 1985 Soviet influence in Africa decreased substantially.

What accounts for the Soviet Union's flagging fortunes in Africa? Three factors have been most important. First, the Soviet Union proved to be a poor patron. As most Soviet analysts now acknowledge, it lacks the skills, capital, and markets necessary to compete effectively with international agencies, multinational corporations, and Western governments in the economic realm. In addition, while Soviet military aid has ensured the short-term survival of the regimes in Angola, Ethiopia, and (to a lesser extent)

*On relations between the Reagan administration and Mozambique, see Clement (1985: 39-44) and Clough and Jordan (1984-85).

†On the Soviet Union's earlier problems in Africa, see Legvold (1970) and Stevens (1976).

Mozambique, it has failed to provide security and stability. Second, by 1978 the easy opportunities for Soviet gains afforded by the collapse of Portuguese colonialism and the fall of Haile Selassie had been exhausted. Finally (as noted), the United States adopted a more active and regionally sensitive policy. Since 1976 U.S. policymakers have endeavored, with surprising and largely unremarked success, to convince African leaders that diplomatically and economically it is the West and not the Soviet bloc which can help Africa solve its problems. In short, in the latter 1970s and early 1980s the regional and international environment became much less conducive to growing Soviet influence in Africa.

THE RISE OF ANTI-COMMUNIST INTERVENTIONISM

In July 1985 the U.S. House of Representatives unexpectedly voted to repeal the Clark Amendment, a nine-year-old ban on covert aid to antigovernment insurgents in Angola. This move was hailed by many Congressmen as a new American willingness to challenge Soviet expansionism. Its timing was somewhat paradoxical given the evidence we have presented that earlier fears of a mounting Soviet threat in Africa had been greatly exaggerated. To understand the upsurge of political support for an aggressively anti-Communist, pro-"freedom" posture in Angola and other African countries it is necessary to look beyond Africa.

Public enthusiasm for Third World "freedom fighters" waging wars of liberation against "Communist" regimes bolstered by the Soviet Union, Cuba, and East Germany is a new phenomenon with diverse roots. The first serious consideration of aid to anti-Communist insurgents came in 1980, following the Soviet invasion of Afghanistan. A limited program of aid to the Afghan resistance was approved by the Carter administration, but it was done on a case-specific basis with no thought of formulating a general strategy or doctrine.* With the election of Ronald Reagan, however, support for a consistent policy of aid to groups opposing radical socialist governments with close ties to the Soviet Union began to build.

During the 1980 presidential campaign, candidate Reagan on several occasions expressed support for the Afghan resistance and for UNITA (*Christian Science Monitor*, 25 June 1980). Shortly

---

*On U.S. covert aid to the Afghan rebels, see *Time*, 11 June 1984.

after the new administration took office, Haig expressed the belief that under certain circumstances aid to such groups was an appropriate counter to Soviet expansion (*Manchester Guardian Weekly*, 29 March 1981). But no policy for such aid was developed. One reason for the lack of such a policy was the determined refusal in late 1981 of the House of Representatives to repeal the Clark Amendment (*New York Times*, 1 October and 15 December 1981). Another reason (as discussed below) was that Haig was persuaded that a policy of unremitting opposition to radical socialist states might increase rather than decrease Soviet influence in the Third World. Even in the Afghan case, the administration decided to limit aid and keep it low key. In late 1982, for example, it opposed moves to put Congress publicly on record in support of aid to the Afghan insurgents (*Congressional Quarterly Almanac* [1982]: 166-67).

President Reagan retained the idea of aggressively challenging Soviet-backed states in the Third World, however, with strong and repeated declarations of support for "the heroic freedom fighters of Afghanistan," and rhetoric such as was included in his address to the British Parliament on 8 June 1982.* Although the issue of aid to anti-Communist insurgents was not addressed directly, the President's ringing call for "a crusade for freedom" clearly established the basis for such a policy. A particularly critical passage was the following:

> We cannot ignore the fact that even without our encouragement there has been and will continue to be repeated explosions against repression and dictatorships. The Soviet Union is not immune to this reality. Any system is inherently unstable that has no peaceful means to legitimize its leaders. In such cases, the very repressiveness of the state ultimately drives people to resist it, if necessary, by force. . . . We must be staunch in our conviction that freedom is not the sole prerogative of a lucky few, but the inalienable and universal right of all human beings (*WCPD:RR* [1982]: 767-68).

In other speeches in 1982 and 1983 Reagan decried the reactive character of past American policies (*Department of State Bulletin*, March 1983: 28) and declared the need for "a forward strategy for freedom" (*WCPD:RR* [1983]: 262). Seizing upon the President's

---

*For example, see *Weekly Compilation of Presidential Documents Administration of Ronald Reagan* (1982: 217, 1644 and 1983: 430). Cited hereafter as *WCPD:RR*.

universalistic rhetoric, conservative analysts began to speak wistfully of a "Reagan doctrine" which would have the United States intervene in support of anti-Communist "freedom fighters" throughout the Third World (for example, see Krauthammer 1985).

Not until early 1985 did the President appear to formally endorse the doctrine that his rhetoric had inspired. In his State of the Union address on 6 February Reagan declared the following:

> Freedom is not the sole prerogative of a chosen few; it is the universal right of all God's children. Our mission is to nourish and defend freedom and democracy and to communicate these ideals everywhere we can. We cannot play innocents abroad in a world that's not innocent, nor can we be passive when freedom is under siege. We must stand by all our democratic allies. And we must not break faith with those who are risking their lives — on every continent, from Afghanistan to Nicaragua — to defy Soviet-supported aggression and secure rights which have been ours from birth (*Department of State Bulletin*, April 1985: 9).

Ten days later, in his weekly radio broadcast, the President referred to "freedom fighters in Afghanistan, Ethiopia, Cambodia, and Angola," and suggestively pointed out that "Time and again in the course of our history, we've aided those around the world struggling for freedom, democracy, independence, and liberation from tyranny" (*Department of State Bulletin*, April 1985: 10). These themes were given their most lengthy and detailed exposition by Secretary of State George Shultz on 22 February 1985. In a speech entitled "America and the Struggle for Freedom," Shultz declared that the United States "has a moral responsibility" to support "popular insurgencies against communist domination"; he made it clear that this meant providing arms to insurgents if necessary (*Department of State Bulletin*, April 1985: 18).

The Reagan administration's rhetoric contrasted sharply with the approach it had been following in its dealings with Africa. After the defeat of efforts to repeal the Clark Amendment in 1981, administration officials began to downplay the UNITA factor and develop a working relationship with the MPLA government in Luanda.*
By 1984 negotiations concerning Namibia and the reduction of the Cuban presence in Angola had reached the point that preliminary preparations were being made for the recognition of the MPLA

---

*For clear statements of the pragmatic character of U.S. policy toward Angola and Mozambique prior to July 1985, see Wisner (1985 and 1984).

government. As Lowenkopf discusses, U.S. relations with Mozambique had improved even more dramatically. In December 1982 the administration turned down a request for aid from anti-Communist insurgents in Ethiopia (D. Ottaway and Omang 1985). Rapprochements with radical socialist governments in the Congo and Benin developed in 1982, and relations with radical governments in Algeria, Guinea-Bissau, and Madagascar warmed considerably (*Africa Contemporary Record*, 1982-83: B210, B378-79, and 1983-84: B11-12, B197, B367-68, B413-14). In addition, immediately after taking office, the Reagan administration opted to maintain the close relationship with the Mugabe government in Zimbabwe that had been fostered by the Carter administration. Haig spelled out the rationale underlying this accommodative approach in June 1981:

> We are acutely conscious of a growing trend in which Third World leaders and Third World people are increasingly leery of close association with the Russian Marxist-Leninist model. . . . We are not about to proceed in our efforts to establish a just and responsible relationship with the developing world in such a way that we will have the practical consequences of reversing this growing favorable trend.
>
> It underlines why the United States was one of the major contributors to Zimbabwe's aid requirements this past year. It underlines why this Administration was the highest donor to the black African refugee conference in Geneva. . . . And it underlines why we are dedicated, within the general framework of U.N. Resolution 435, to seek an independent, internationally recognized Namibia (*Department of State Bulletin*, July 1981: 19).

In a similar vein, Haig told a group of newspaper editors in April 1981 that "We must offer hope that the United States and its allies are not some form of closed club, hostile to the problems and frustrations attending development" (*Department of State Bulletin*, June 1981: 7). One year later, Haig was cautiously optimistic that the pragmatic approach was working:

> Beneath the surface, new opportunities for economic and political cooperation with the West are being seized by individual Third World states in ever more practical ways. . . . Such a situation calls for sensitivity and sophistication on our part if we are to expand our links with developing countries. We hold all sovereign states responsible for what they say and do. But we must also recognize the complex equations of economic and political survival

in developing nations. Neither we nor they can afford ideological stereotypes in cases where they do not fit (*Department of State Bulletin*, June 1982: 42).

These remarks reflected the administration's decision in 1981 to pursue a policy far more nuanced and less doctrinaire than that suggested by the Reagan and Shultz declarations of 1985. Conservative ideologues, who discerned a difference between these two approaches, have campaigned from the beginning of the administration against "State Department pragmatists" who were preventing Reagan from being Reagan in Africa and elsewhere.*

In 1985 the conservative globalist assault on the Reagan administration's pragmatic policies toward Africa began to gain momentum. Several factors increased support for a more ideological and confrontational policy. A steady escalation of the administration's campaign against the Sandinista government in Nicaragua was especially important in undercutting Crocker's efforts to carry out rapprochements with Mozambique and Angola. Why, many Congressmen asked, did it make sense to support "freedom fighters" in Nicaragua but not in Mozambique and in Angola? During hearings on the 1986 foreign assistance bill, Congressman Steven Solarz put the following to a State Department official:

> Lately the President has been saying that we have a moral obligation to provide military assistance to the freedom fighters who are battling the Marxist-Leninist regime in Nicaragua, presumably on behalf of the ideals of democracy which gave birth to our own revolution. Yet in Mozambique, instead of providing military assistance to RENAMO, which claims to be fighting in the name of democracy against the Marxist regime, we are helping the government. Now . . . could you explain to me what is the justification for providing military assistance to the contras but not to RENAMO, if they are both fighting against Marxist governments in favor of democracy? (United States 1985).

The inability of administration officials to provide a convincing answer to that question was a major reason for the gradual extension of the "Reagan doctrine" to Africa.

---

*For example, see "Why Is Chester Crocker Trying to Sell 20 Million Black Africans into Communist Slavery?"; advertisement, *Washington Times*, 7 December 1984; "The Shultz Doctrine and Mozambique," *Washington Times*, 1 March 1985; Heritage Foundation (1985); and Republican Study Committee (1985).

CONCLUSION: COMING TO TERMS WITH RADICAL SOCIALISM

The failure of the Crocker team to deliver a long promised settlement in southern Africa—combining plans to bring independence to Namibia and reduce the Cuban military presence in Angola—also contributed substantially to the erosion of support for a pragmatic Africa policy (Clough and Jordan 1984-85 and Clough 1985-86). Without clear-cut administration successes to legitimate a policy of "constructive engagement," the policy came under increasing attack from both sides of the political spectrum.

If Congress had not repealed the Clark Amendment, Crocker and his supporters might have been able to stave off challenges from ideologically minded conservatives within the administration. Once the amendment was repealed, however, policy shifted quickly. By late November President Reagan was openly supporting aid to UNITA (*New York Times,* 23 November 1985). In a departure from previous policy, administration officials appear to have made the inclusion of Savimbi in a coalition Angolan government a condition of a settlement involving Angola and Namibia (*Washington Post,* 27 November 1985).

The sudden upsurge of support for the "Reagan doctrine" manifested itself in July 1985 Congressional votes to aid insurgents in Nicaragua, Cambodia, and Afghanistan; to repeal the Clark Amendment; and to block military aid to Mozambique (*Congressional Quarterly,* 13 July 1985: 1359-63; see also Greenberger 1985). It resulted from a convergence of four groups:

1. Symbolic interventionists, most of whom (like Claude Pepper) are Democratic politicians who find such a posture electorally attractive. It allows them to appear tough on communism and identify with the cause of "freedom" without (they hope) paying a high price.*
2. Conservative regionalists who believe that supporting opponents of the governments in Angola, Ethiopia, and (possibly) Mozambique is the best way to pressure these governments to temper their ideological posture, accommodate their internal rivals, and limit their ties to the Soviets.
3. Ideological globalists, like Jeane Kirkpatrick, Congressman Jack Kemp, and (most likely) President Reagan, who believe that the United States can and must seize the moral high

---

*On Democratic concerns about appearing tough on the Soviets, see Solarz (1985). It should be noted, however, that Solarz has consistently opposed aid to UNITA.

ground by supporting "freedom fighters" throughout the Third World who are struggling against the imposition of "Soviet-style totalitarianism."*

4. Cynical globalists, who see support of "freedom fighters" in Angola and elsewhere as a means of bogging Moscow down in costly and interminable conflicts in the periphery which will at least prevent the Soviets from making further gains in the Third World and might at best increase internal "contradictions" in the Soviet Union, thus contributing to the decay of the Communist system (Pipes 1984).

It would be dangerous and misleading to construe the convergence of these groups as evidence of a new strategic consensus, however. As the debate shifts from relatively soft choices (such as whether to repeal the Clark Amendment), to harder choices (such as whether to provide limited amounts of aid to groups such as UNITA), and ultimately to extremely hard choices (such as whether to intervene decisively on behalf of embattled insurgents in the face of escalating and determined Soviet support for incumbent governments), cleavages among the four groups are likely to emerge.† Rising costs and growing risks will inevitably cause the ardor of some supporters of the "Reagan doctrine" to cool—especially the symbolic interventionists. In addition, disagreements are certain to break out between conservative regionalists, who are pursuing limited regional objectives (such as lessening the MPLA's ties with Moscow and Havana), and ideological globalists, who want nothing short of victory for "the forces of freedom" and would oppose any deal that "sold out" pro-Western allies. Cynical globalists (who are probably most responsible for the increased enthusiasm within the Reagan administration for aid to UNITA) are likely to come into conflict eventually with both conservative regionalists, whose policies, if successful, would create stable situations that would no longer drain Soviet resources, and ideological globalists, who might overcommit U.S. resources and thus bog down the United States as much as the Soviet Union. Thus this coalition is inherently unstable. More important, pursuing the policies advocated by these groups will be dangerous and counterproductive.

*In addition to previous references regarding the views of Reagan and Kirkpatrick, see Podhoretz (1976, 1980, and 1981); Kristol (1985); Gingrich (1985: 5614-18); and Kemp (1985).

†For evidence that such a process has already begun, see Roberts (1985).

CONCLUSION: COMING TO TERMS WITH RADICAL SOCIALISM 85

THE SOURCES OF SOVIET INFLUENCE

The case for aiding anti-Communist insurgents in Africa rests on a mistaken understanding of the factors that determine the alignments of radical socialist states, and hence the nature of Soviet influence in the Third World. On the basis of false analogies with the rise of communism in the Soviet Union and Eastern Europe, some conservative globalists have attempted to explain Third World alignments with the Soviet Union in terms of Soviet "penetration" and "subversion" (for example, see Bissell 1979). Such arguments cannot be reconciled with events in any African country. From Egypt and Guinea in the 1950s to Angola, Mozambique, and Ethiopia in the 1970s, every African country that has become an ally of the Soviet Union has done so as a result of a conscious and unforced decision. Before such a decision, the Soviet presence in most of these countries was minimal at most. To explain why independent African leaders, many of whom (such as Mengistu) lacked a prior ideological affinity with the Soviet Union, choose to associate with the Communist camp requires an understanding of the so-called "natural ally" thesis.

Repeatedly invoked by Soviet officials, the natural ally thesis holds that the Soviet Union and radical socialist states in the Third World share a common project—building socialism—and a common enemy—capitalist imperialism. Brutents, for example, has written as follows:

> It is certain that in future, support from the Soviet Union, the socialist countries and the international working-class movement will continue as always to be vital to the national liberation struggle. Without this support it is impossible to ultimately defeat neo-colonialism and advance along the road of social progress. Without this support it would be impossible to ensure that the developing countries' growing international authority is a stable process (1979: 275).

This thesis has both a positive and a negative thread. The positive strand—the claim that the Soviet Union and radical socialist states share a commitment to building socialism—has only a limited and fading appeal for most Third World leaders. Far more important is the negative strand, which holds that the Soviet Union is the only reliable source of protection against capitalist imperialism, regional aggression, and internal subversion. In a typical statement of this position, one Soviet analyst, L. A. Alekseyev, wrote that: "The economic, political and military might of the Soviet Union and the socialist commonwealth is the main deterrent factor to neocolonial strivings of imperialist states, their expansionist encroachments" (1978: 62). In 1977 Brezhnev had stressed the same point:

> The socialist countries are staunch and reliable friends of . . . countries [of socialist orientation] and are prepared to give them the utmost assistance and support in the development along the progressive path. This means not only moral and political, but also economic and organizational support including assistance in strengthening their defenses (1978: 33).

When Third World leaders have embraced the natural ally thesis, they have almost without exception been motivated by such promises of support. In their own explications of the thesis, they invariably stress the negative strand. In 1979, for example, Machel referred to the socialist countries as "a reliable rearguard for the victory of our liberation struggle," calling them the "natural ally for the defense of our political and economic independence" (quoted in Rothenberg 1980: 118). According to a 1978 FRELIMO party document, "Political alliance with the socialist countries constitutes an important strategic factor for dissuasion of the aggressive plans of imperialism (quoted in Ottaway and Ottaway 1981: 179).

A necessary corollary of the natural ally thesis is that a "natural antagonism" exists between the United States and radical socialist governments in the Third World. Whether correct or not, a belief that the United States is fundamentally opposed to regimes that embrace radical socialism has been a prime consideration in the decision of many such regimes to tilt toward the Eastern bloc. In a world dominated by two superpowers, the perception that one of the superpowers is fundamentally hostile will—in accord with the familiar principle that "the enemy of my enemy is my friend"—inevitably cause states to seek the support of the other superpower.

Western conservatives often distort this corollary by attempting to establish that its premise—that the United States is a threat to radical socialist states—is false. (Paradoxically, they usually so argue at the same time that they are advocating the adoption of policies that would threaten such states.) For example, President Reagan, Jeane Kirkpatrick, and other strident critics of the Sandinistas in Nicaragua constantly claim that U.S. policy was not initially hostile to the revolution and that it is therefore implausible to argue that Nicaragua's decision to develop close ties with Moscow could have been motivated by defense considerations.*

The Reagan/Kirkpatrick argument is ironic because Reagan and Kirkpatrick have consistently stressed that conflict between radical socialist ("Marxist"/"totalitarian"/"terrorist") states and the United States is inevitable. Indeed the argument is a central thesis of an article which earned Kirkpatrick Reagan's favor—and a job as U.S. Ambassador to the United Nations (Kirkpatrick 1979). Writings such as this article and statements such as those cited above by Reagan give credibility to the natural ally thesis and as a result boost Soviet prospects in the Third World.

In the mid-1970s many if not most radical socialist Third World leaders perceived the United States as a potential adversary. From their vantage point, American interventions in Iran, Guatemala, Lebanon, Cuba, the Dominican Republic, the Congo (Kinshasa), Southeast Asia, and Chile provided ample grounds for such an assessment (Barnet 1968; Packenham 1973; Krasner 1978). At independence the governments in Luanda and Maputo had more immediate reasons for concern. Based on the Ford administration's abortive intervention in the Angolan civil war in 1975, they were understandably fearful that the United States would work in concert with South Africa to subvert their governments. Similarly, candidate Reagan's virulent attacks on the "appeasement" policies of the Carter administration increased Nicaraguan doubts that the United States would continue to pursue an accommodationist approach.† To admit that Third World leaders have some justification for their concerns does not require that one agree that there is a natural antagonism between the United States and radical socialist states in the Third World. Nor does it involve simply blaming the United States for conflicts with such states. If we are to understand the

---

*For example, see Kirkpatrick's (1983: 71-74) reply to Nicaraguan charges of U.S. aggression.

†It is important here to draw a distinction between understanding why someone holds a particular view and agreeing with that view. I do not share the view of some liberal analysts (e.g., Barnet, Packenham, and Krasner) that in the postwar era the United States has consistently opposed revolutionary change and radical socialist governments. However, it is absurd to argue, as Kirkpatrick and other conservative globalists do, that Third World leaders' fears of U.S. intervention are groundless, deriving entirely from radical paranoia, ideological anti-Americanism, and Soviet propaganda. It is also intellectually dishonest given that conservative globalists urge the adoption of policies in Angola, Nicaragua, Mozambique, and elsewhere that would threaten radical socialist regimes.

factors influencing Third World alignments, we must recognize that previous U.S. policies and current actions, as well as public rhetoric, (official and unofficial), all have an effect on Third World leaders' perceptions of their international options.

Since the end of World War II, Third World states have frequently reversed their alliance orientations (see "Soviet Geopolitical Momentum: Myth or Menace?" *Defense Monitor,* January 1980). U.S. policymakers must determine which strategy, if any, is most effective in causing shifts to the West. Based on the evidence presented above, a strong case can be made that an accommodative strategy is the best approach. By discrediting the negative strand of the natural ally thesis, this strategy significantly undercut Moscow's position in Africa. Thus now is not a time to change strategy — especially if the alternative is the "Reagan doctrine."

IMPLICATIONS OF APPLYING THE "REAGAN DOCTRINE" TO AFRICA

By attempting to force radical socialist states to make a hard choice* between the Soviet Union and the United States and between socialism and capitalism, extension of the "Reagan doctrine" to Africa would give renewed credibility to the negative strand of the natural ally thesis and its natural adversary corollary. This would cause a number of states to seek closer ties with the Soviet Union. At the same time, the highly visible challenge this doctrine presents to the Soviet Union's status as a global power would stiffen Moscow's resolve, especially in Angola and Ethiopia. As a result, the United States could be forced to make a very difficult and politically divisive choice between retreating and leaving the Soviet Union in a stronger position on the continent, on the one hand, and significantly escalating the level of U.S. military involvement there, on the other hand.

Using aid to insurgents to change the composition and/or behavior of radical socialist regimes will work only under certain

---

*Kenneth Jowitt defines the degree of choices as follows: *"Hard choices* are those demanding an either-or response to the practical (i.e., strategic and policy (implications of their formal ideological commitments; *easy choices* are those that allow an elite to avoid understanding and acting on the practical implications of their formal ideological commitments (1979: 150-51). Put differently, imposing hard choices on Third World states would involve forcing them to pay a higher price for radical rhetoric and relations with the Soviet Union; in economic terms, it would mean raising the opportunity costs of such behavior.

conditions. First, if a conservative regionalist strategy is adopted, the changes demanded must be changes that the incumbent regime, or at least a substantial faction within that regime, is willing (albeit very reluctantly) to accept. Second, the regime being threatened must be persuaded that pressure will not abate until the demanded changes have been made. Finally, that regime must lack the means to resist effectively.

Whether or not the first condition can be met in the Angolan, Ethiopian, and Mozambican cases will depend on which view of American objectives is favored by the Reagan administration. None of these three states would be willing to satisfy the maximalist demands of ideological globalists—i.e., the creation of a Western democratic political system providing for immediate elections and a total break with the Eastern bloc. Angola and Mozambique have been consistently willing to satisfy the minimalist demands of conservative regionalists—i.e., negotiated settlements of regional disputes and reductions in the Eastern bloc's military presence—provided such concessions did not leave them vulnerable to their internal or external adversaries. But both ideological and cynical globalists have resisted such deals. For example, in early 1985 the ranking Republican on the House Foreign Affairs Subcommittee on Africa, Congressman Mark Siljander, expressed the globalist view: "Why should we be supporting Mozambique militarily when there is a victory against a Marxist government in sight, just because they happen to be kow-towing to the United States a bit in the midst of their decline and fall?" (United States 1985). Internal agreements that would incorporate insurgents into the existing regimes in these countries are desirable, but they are very unlikely. As Marcum and Henze demonstrate, neither the MPLA nor the Derg is likely to agree to a coalition government that would give their internal foes real power. Machel and FRELIMO might agree to a coalition, but only on their own terms. If anything, support for antigovernment insurgents would make Luanda, Addis Ababa, and Maputo more insecure and intransigent.

Whether or not the second condition can be met will depend on American domestic politics. Given the shaky nature of the coalition favoring the "Reagan doctrine" and the relatively low priority attached to Africa by most officials and opinion leaders, there is good reason to doubt that the administration will commit substantial resources over an extended period to pressure Angola and Ethiopia. Moreover, in the Angolan case support for Savimbi will unavoidably require cooperation with South Africa and will thus be certain to intensify domestic opposition. Aiding anti-Communist insurgents will remain popular only so long as it either stays cheap or scores quick victories.

Soviet reactions to the extension of the "Reagan doctrine" to Africa will ensure that such a policy will neither stay cheap nor score quick successes. Africa is not among Moscow's global priorities, nor do Soviet leaders seem inclined to commit significant resources to achieve new successes on the continent. However, they cannot allow either the MPLA or the Derg to be defeated by Western-backed insurgents. Soviet officials, publicists, and academics have consistently sought to communicate this message to the United States since at least 1983. For example, in late 1983 Soviet officials at the United Nations warned South African officials that Moscow would not allow the MPLA to be defeated militarily by UNITA (*Washington Post*, 5 January 1984). "In view of the friendly nature of Soviet-Angolan relations," a Soviet official later commented, "[the Soviet Union] cannot be indifferent to the problem of Angola's security" (Moscow, June 1984). The marked increase in the level and sophistication of Soviet support for the MPLA since the 1983 warning to South Africa provides good reason to take these statements seriously (*Sunday Times*, 29 September 1985). Moreover, there is no evidence that under pressure the Soviets will desert radical socialist countries with which they have established security ties.

Conservative globalists ought to understand better than most Americans why Soviet leaders are unlikely to back down in Angola and Ethiopia. Moscow's fears concerning the possible global repercussions of defeats in these two symbolically important countries derive from the same concerns about credibility that underlay the "domino theory" with which U.S. officials used to rationalize an escalating U.S. commitment to defend South Vietnam.*

Supporting anti-Communist insurgents will not advance democracy or end regional instability. Instead it is most likely to embitter existing socialist regimes and enhance the credibility of the natural ally thesis. It is also likely to ensure that opposition forces in South Africa will move closer to Moscow in anticipation of an "inevitable" conflict with the United States. For all of these reasons, extending the Reagan doctrine to Africa could reverse recent declines in Soviet influence on the continent.

*On the ways in which concern for credibility have affected U.S. policy in the Third World, see Price (1978: 32-35) and Gelb with Betts (1979).

APPENDIX

AGREEMENT

ON NON-AGGRESSION AND GOOD NEIGHBOURLINESS

BETWEEN

THE GOVERNMENT OF
THE PEOPLE'S REPUBLIC OF MOZAMBIQUE

AND

THE GOVERNMENT OF
THE REPUBLIC OF SOUTH AFRICA

The Government of the People's Republic of Mozambique and the Government of the Republic of South Africa, hereinafter referred to as the High Contracting Parties;

RECOGNISING the principles of strict respect for sovereignty and territorial integrity, sovereign equality, political independence and the inviolability of the borders of all states;

REAFFIRMING the principle of non-interference in the internal affairs of other states;

CONSIDERING the internationally recognised principle of the right of peoples to self-determination and independence and the principle of equal rights of all peoples;

CONSIDERING the obligation of all states to refrain, in their international relations, from the threat or use of force against the territorial integrity or political independence of any state;

CONSIDERING the obligation of states to settle conflicts by peaceful means, and thus safeguard international peace and security and justice;

RECOGNISING the responsibility of states not to allow their territory to be used for acts of war, aggression or violence against other states;

CONSCIOUS of the need to promote relations of good neighbourliness based on the principles of equality of rights and mutual advantage;

CONVINCED that relations of good neighbourliness between the High Contracting Parties will contribute to peace, security, stability and progress in Southern Africa, the Continent and the World;

Have solemnly agreed to the following:

ARTICLE ONE

The High Contracting Parties undertake to respect each other's sovereignty and independence and, in fulfilment of this fundamental obligation, to refrain from interfering in the internal affairs of the other.

ARTICLE TWO

(1) The High Contracting Parties shall resolve differences and disputes that may arise between them and that may or are likely to endanger mutual peace and security or peace and security in the region, by means of negotiation, enquiry, mediation, conciliation, arbitration or other peaceful means, and undertake not to resort, individually or collectively, to the threat or use of force against each other's sovereignty, territorial integrity or political independence.

(2) For the purposes of this article, the use of force shall include *inter alia* —
  (a) attacks by land, air or sea forces;
  (b) sabotage;
  (c) unwarranted concentration of such forces at or near the international boundaries of the High Contracting Parties;
  (d) violation of the international land, air or sea boundaries of either of the High Contracting Parties.

(3) The High Contracting Parties shall not in any way assist the armed forces of any state or group of states deployed against the territorial sovereignty or political independence of the other.

ARTICLE THREE

(1) The High Contracting Parties shall not allow their respective territories, territorial waters or air space to be used as a base, thoroughfare, or in any other way by another state, government, foreign military forces, organisations or individuals which plan or prepare to commit acts of violence, terrorism or aggression against the territorial integrity or political independence of the other or may threaten the security of its inhabitants.

(2) The High Contracting Parties, in order to prevent or eliminate the acts or the preparation of acts mentioned in paragraph (1) of this article, undertake in particular to—
  (a) forbid and prevent in their respective territories the organisation of irregular forces or armed bands, including mercenaries, whose objective is to carry out the acts contemplated in paragraph (1) of this article;
  (b) eliminate from their respective territories bases, training centres, places of shelter, accommodation and transit for elements who intend to carry out the acts contemplated in paragraph (1) of this article;
  (c) eliminate from their respective territories centres or depots containing armaments of whatever nature, destined to be used by the elements contemplated in paragraph (1) of this article;
  (d) eliminate from their respective territories command posts or other places for the command, direction and co-ordination of the elements contemplated in paragraph (1) of this article;
  (e) eliminate from their respective territories communication and telecommunication facilities between the command and the elements contemplated in paragraph (1) of this article;
  (f) eliminate and prohibit the installation in their respective territories of radio broadcasting stations, including unofficial or clandestine broadcasts, for the elements that carry out the acts contemplated in paragraph (1) of this article;

(g) exercise strict control, in their respective territories, over elements which intend to carry out or plan the acts contemplated in paragraph (1) of this article;

(h) prevent the transit of elements who intend or plan to commit the acts contemplated in paragraph (1) of this article, from a place in the territory of either to a place in the territory of the other or to a place in the territory of any third state which has a common boundary with the High Contracting Party against which such elements intend or plan to commit the said acts;

(i) take appropriate steps in their respective territories to prevent the recruitment of elements of whatever nationality for the purpose of carrying out the acts contemplated in paragraph (1) of this article;

(j) prevent the elements contemplated in paragraph (1) of this article from carrying out from their respective territories by any means acts of abduction or other acts, aimed at taking citizens of any nationality hostage in the territory of the other High Contracting Party; and

(k) prohibit the provision on their respective territories of any logistic facilities for carrying out the acts contemplated in paragraph (1) of this article.

(3) The High Contracting Parties will not use the territory of third states to carry out or support the acts contemplated in paragraphs (1) and (2) of this article.

ARTICLE FOUR

The High Contracting Parties shall take steps, individually and collectively, to ensure that the international boundary between their respective territories is effectively patrolled and that the border posts are efficiently administered to prevent illegal crossings from the territory of a High Contracting Party to the territory of the other, and in particular, by elements contemplated in Article Three of this Agreement.

ARTICLE FIVE

The High Contracting Parties shall prohibit within their territory acts of propaganda that incite a war of aggression against the other High Contracting Party and shall also prohibit acts of propaganda aimed at inciting acts of terrorism and civil war in the territory of the other High Contracting Party.

ARTICLE SIX

The High Contracting Parties declare that there is no conflict between their commitments in treaties and international obligations and the commitments undertaken in this Agreement.

ARTICLE SEVEN

The High Contracting Parties are committed to interpreting this Agreement in good faith and will maintain periodic contact to ensure the effective application of what has been agreed.

ARTICLE EIGHT

Nothing in this Agreement shall be construed as detracting from the High Contracting Parties' right of self-defence in the event of armed attacks, as provided for in the Charter of the United Nations.

ARTICLE NINE

(1) Each of the High Contracting Parties shall appoint high-ranking representatives to serve on a Joint Security Commission with the aim of supervising and monitoring the application of this Agreement.

(2) The Commission shall determine its own working procedure.

(3) The Commission shall meet on a regular basis and may be specially convened whenever circumstances so require.

(4) The Commission shall —
   (a) Consider all allegations of infringements of the provisions of this Agreement;
   (b) advise the High Contracting Parties of its conclusions; and
   (c) make recommendations to the High Contracting Parties concerning measures for the effective application of this Agreement and the settlement of disputes over infringements or alleged infringements.

(5) The High Contracting Parties shall determine the mandate of their respective representatives in order to enable interim measures to be taken in cases of duly recognised emergency.

(6) The High Contracting Parties shall make available all the facilities necessary for the effective functioning of the Commission and will jointly consider its conclusions and recommendations.

ARTICLE TEN

This Agreement will also be known as "The Accord of Nkomati".

ARTICLE ELEVEN

(1) This Agreement shall enter into force on the date of the signature thereof.

(2) Any amendment to this Agreement agreed to by the High Contracting Parties shall be effected by the Exchange of Notes between them.

IN WITNESS WHEREOF, the signatories, in the name of their respective governments, have signed and sealed this Agreement, in quadruplicate in the Portuguese and English languages, both texts being equally authentic.

THUS DONE AND SIGNED AT the common border on the banks of the Nkomati River, on this the sixteenth day of March 1984.

SAMORA MOISÉS MACHEL
Marshal of the Republic
President of the People's
Republic of Mozambique
President of the Council
of Ministers

PIETER WILLEM BOTHA
Prime Minister of the
Republic of South Africa

For the Government of the
People's Republic of
Mozambique

For the Government of the
Republic of South Africa

BIBLIOGRAPHY

Albright, David E. 1983. *The USSR and Sub-Saharan Africa in the 1980s.* New York: Praeger.

Albright, David E., ed. 1980. *Communism in Africa.* Bloomington: Indiana University Press.

Alekseyev, L.A. 1978. *Africa: Struggle for Political and Economic Liberation.* Moscow: Znanie.

Alexiev, Alex. 1982. "Soviet Strategy in the Third World and Nicaragua." Santa Monica, Calif.: Rand Corporation.

de Almeida, Roberto. 1986. Interview in *AfricAsia*, no. 25 (January).

de Andrade, Mário. 1960. "Et les colonies de Salazar?" *Démocratie nouvelle* (Paris) 14, 9 (September).

————. 1966. "Le Mouvement de libération dans les colonies portugaises." *Partisans* (Paris), nos. 29-30 (May-June).

de Andrade, Mário, and Ollivier, Marc. 1971. *La Guerre en Angola: Etude socioéconomique.* Paris: François Maspero.

Barnet, Richard. 1968. *Intervention and Revolution.* New York: New American Library.

Bender, Gerald. 1978. "Angola, the Cubans, and American Anxieties." *Foreign Policy* (Summer): 7-8.

————. 1981. "Kissinger in Angola: Anatomy of Failure." In *American Policy in Southern Africa: The Stakes and the Stance*, ed. René Lemarchand. Washington, D.C.: University Press of America.

Bienen, Henry. 1982. "Soviet Political Relations with Africa." *International Security* (Spring).

Bissell, Richard. 1979. "Soviet Policies in Africa." *Current History* (October).

Brezhnev, L.I. 1978. Speech on the sixtieth anniversary of the revolution, 2 November 1977. *Survival* (January-February): 33.

Brind, Harry. 1983-84. "Soviet Policy in the Horn of Africa." *International Affairs* (Winter).

Brittain, Victoria. 1984. "Angola Learns to Live with Perpetual War." *Guardian* (London), 19 October.

Brutents, Karen. 1979. *The Newly Free Countries in the Seventies.* Moscow: Progress Publishers.

Campbell, Horace. 1984. "War, Reconstruction and Dependence in Mozambique." *Third World Quarterly* (October).

Carvalho Santos, Henrique de—"Onambwe" (Minister of Industry). 1984. Speech at MPLA party meeting in Malange. Quoted in *Guardian*, 19 October.

Chaliand, Gerard. 1982. *The Struggle for Africa*. New York: St. Martin's Press.

Clapham, Christopher. 1969. *Haile Selassie's Government*. New York: Praeger; London: Longmans.

Clement, Peter. 1985. "Moscow and Southern Africa." *Problems of Communism* (March-April).

Clough, Michael. 1980. "The Mugabe Landslide." *African Index*, 7 March.

———. 1983. "Whither Zimbabwe?" *CSIS Africa Notes*, 15 November.

———. 1984. "Exploring Afrocommunism." *Problems of Communism* (November-December).

———. 1985. "The UN: A Not So Dangerous Place?" *CSIS Africa Notes* 24 July.

———. 1985-86. "Beyond Constructive Engagement." *Foreign Policy* (Winter).

Clough, Michael, and Jordan, Donald. 1984-85. "The United States and Africa 1984." *Africa Contemporary Record*.

Cohen, John. 1984. "Agrarian Reform in Ethiopia, the Situation on the Eve of the Revolution's 10th Anniversary." Cambridge, Mass.: Harvard Institute for International Development; Development Paper no. 164 (April).

Crocker, Chester A. 1986. "The U.S. and Angola." *Current Policy*, no. 796 18 (February). U.S. Department of State, Bureau of Public Affairs.

da Cruz, Viriato. 1962. "O futuro dos Brancos em Angola." In *Angola atravès dos textos*. São Paulo: Editora Felman-Rego.

———. 1964. "What Kind of Independence for Angola?" *Révolution* (Paris) 1, 9 (January).

David, Stephen. 1979. "Realignment in the Horn." *International Security* (Fall).

Davidow, Jeffrey. 1984. *A Peace in Southern Africa*. Boulder, Colo.: Westview Press.

Davidson, Basil; Cliffe, Lionel; and Selassie, Bereket Habte, eds. 1980. *Behind the War in Eritrea*. Nottingham, England: Spokesman.

Diallo Siradiou. 1985. "L'Angola avant-poste de l'Afrique." *Jeune Afrique*, 7 August: 31.

dos Santos, Jose Eduardo. 1985a. Speech to the National Party Conference, 14 January. In U.S. Department of Commerce, Foreign Broadcast Information Service (FBIS), Southern Africa, 15 January, p. U2.

———. 1985b. Report at MPLA-PT Party Congress, 2 December. In FBIS, 5 December, p. U3.

Durch, William. 1978. "The Cuban Military in Africa and the Middle East: From Algeria to Angola." *Studies in Comparative Communism* (Spring-Summer).

Ebinger, Charles. 1984. *Foreign Intervention in Civil War.* Boulder, Colo.: Westview Press.

Erlich, Haggai. 1983. "Eritrea and the 1974 Revolution in Ethiopia." In Erlich, *The Struggle over Eritrea*, pp. 43-54. Stanford: Hoover Institution.

Etzold, Thomas, and Gaddis, John. 1978. *Containment: Documents on American Policy and Strategy, 1945-1950.* New York: Columbia University Press.

Farer, Thomas. 1979. *War Clouds on the Horn of Africa*, 2d ed. New York: Carnegie Endowment for International Peace.

Feinberg, Richard. 1983. *The Intemperate Zone.* New York: W.W. Norton.

Fukuyama, Frances. 1979. "A New Soviet Strategy." *Commentary* (October).

—————. 1984. *The New Marxist-Leninist States in the Third World.* Santa Monica, Calif.: Rand Corporation (September).

Funk, Gerald. 1985. "Can Ethiopia Survive Both Communism and the Drought?" *CSIS Africa Notes*, 15 March.

Garthoff, Raymond. 1985. *Detente and Confrontation.* Washington, D.C.: Brookings Institution.

Gelb, Leslie, with Richard Betts. 1979. *The Irony of Vietnam: The System Worked.* Washington, D.C.: Brookings Institution.

Gingrich, Newt. 1985. "The Failure of the U.S. State Department." *Congressional Record*, 11 July.

Greenberger, Robert. 1985. "Right-Wing Groups Join in Capitol Hill Crusade to Help Savimbi's Anti-Communists in Angola." *Wall Street Journal*, 25 November.

Gregory, Martyn. 1981. "Zimbabwe 1980: Politicisation through Armed Struggle and Electoral Mobilisation." *Journal of Commonwealth and Comparative Studies.*

Grimmett, Richard. 1984. "Trends in Conventional Arms Transfers to the Third World by Major Supplier, 1976-1983." Congressional Research Service Report No. 84-82F, 7 May.

Gromyko, Anatoli. 1983. *Africa Today: Progress, Difficulties, Perspectives.* Moscow: USSR Academy of Sciences.

—————. 1984. "Socialist Orientation in Africa." In *The Ideology of African Revolutionary Democracy*, ed. "Social Sciences Today" Editorial Board. Moscow: USSR Academy of Sciences.

Gromyko, Anatoli, ed. 1981. *Sovremennye problemy i vneshnyaya politika Efiopii.* Moscow: Mezhdunarodnye Otnosheniya.

Hahn, Walter, and Cottrell, Alvin. 1977. *Soviet Shadow over Africa.* Miami: Center for Advanced International Studies.

Halliday, Fred, and Molyneux, Maxine. 1981. *The Ethiopian Revolution.* New York: Schocken; London: Verso.

Hanks, Robert. 1983. *Southern Africa and Western Security.* Cambridge, Mass.: Institute for Foreign Policy Analysis.

Hanlon, Joseph. 1984. *Mozambique: Revolution under Fire.* London: Zed Press.

Harden, Blaine. 1985. "Playing Games with Starvation." *Washington Post*, 2 June.

Harding, Neil. 1981. "What Does It Mean to Call a Regime Marxist?" In *Marxist Governments*, vol. 1, ed. Bogdan Szajkowski. London: Macmillan.

Heimer, F.W. 1979. *The Decolonization Conflict in Angola, 1974-76: An Essay in Political Sociology*. Geneva: Institut Universitaire des Hautes Etudes Internationales.

Henriksen, Thomas. 1979. *Mozambique: A History*. London: Rex Collings.

_____. 1981. "Communism, Communist States and Africa." In Henriksen, ed.

_____. 1983. "The USSR and Africa: Challenge and Prospects." *Survey* (Autumn-Winter).

Henriksen, Thomas, ed. 1981. *Communist Powers and Sub-Saharan Africa*. Stanford: Hoover Institution.

Henze, Paul. 1981. "Communism and Ethiopia." *Problems of Communism* (May-June): 55-74.

_____. 1982. "Arming the Horn, 1960-1980." Washington, D.C.: Smithsonian Institution; Wilson Center Working Paper. Subsequently published in *The Proceedings of the VIIth International Ethiopian Studies Conference*. Lund, Sweden, 1984.

_____. 1983a. "Getting a Grip on the Horn: The Emergence of the Soviet Presence and Future Prospects." In *The Pattern of Soviet Conduct in the Third World*, ed. Walter Z. Laqueur. New York: Praeger.

_____. 1983b. *Russians and the Horn*. Marina del Rey, Calif.: European American Institute for Security Research; EAI paper no. 5.

_____. 1984a. "Empire in Ferment." *Wilson Quarterly* (Winter): 118-24. Last section of a three-part article on Ethiopia.

_____. 1984b. "Ethiopia Marches to Marxist Drummer but with Western Flair." *Christian Science Monitor*, 24 May.

_____. 1985. *Communist Ethiopia—Is It Succeeding?* Santa Monica, Calif.: Rand Corporation; P-7054 (January).

Heritage Foundation. 1985. "New U.S. Options in Angola and Namibia." Executive Memorandum no. 85, 5 July.

Iman, Zafar. 1983. "Soviet Treaties with Third World Countries." *Soviet Studies* (January).

Isaacman, Allan, and Isaacman, Barbara. 1982. "Mozambique: South Africa's Hidden War." *Africa Report* 27, 6 (November-December).

_____, and _____. 1983a. *Mozambique: From Colonialism to Revolution, 1900-1982*. Boulder, Colo.: Westview Press.

_____, and _____. 1983b. "Mozambique: In Pursuit of Nonalignment." *Africa Report* 28, 3 (May-June).

Jordan, Donald. 1985. "Changing American Assessments of the Soviet Threat in Africa, 1975-1985." Master's thesis, Naval Postgraduate School (December).

Jowitt, Kenneth. 1979. "Scientific Socialist Regimes in Africa: Political Differentiation, Avoidance, and Unawareness." In Rosberg and Callaghy, eds.

Kalter, Joanmarie. 1984. "Mozambique's Peace with South Africa." *Africa Report* 29, 3 (May-June).

Kautsky, John. 1973. "Comparative Communism versus Comparative Politics." *Studies in Comparative Communism* (Spring-Summer).

Keller, Edward. 1985. "Revolutionary Ethiopia: Ideology, Capacity and the Limits of State Autonomy." *Journal of Commonwealth and Comparative Politics* (July).

Kemp, Jack. 1985. "Foreign Policy Agenda." *Washington Quarterly* (Spring).

el-Khawas, Mohamed A., and Cohen, Barry, eds. 1976. *The Kissinger Study of Southern Africa*. Westport, Conn.: Lawrence Hill.

Kiracofe, Charles. 1982. "The Communist Takeover of Angola." *Journal of Social, Political, and Economic Studies* (Winter).

Kirkpatrick, Jeane. 1979. "Dictatorships and Double Standards." *Commentary* (November).

_____. 1983. Comment in *Department of State Bulletin*.

_____. 1985. "Anti-Communist Insurgency and American Policy." *The National Interest* (Fall).

Kitchen, Helen. 1979. "Options for U.S. Policy Toward Africa." *AEI Foreign Policy and Defense Review*, no. 1.

_____. 1983. *U.S. Interests in Africa*. New York: Praeger.

Kitchen, Helen, and Clough, Michael. 1984. *The United States and South Africa: Realities and Red Herrings*. Washington, D.C.: Center for Strategic and International Studies.

Klinghoffer, Arthur. 1980. *The Angolan War*. Boulder, Colo.: Westview Press.

Kokorev, Vladimir. 1979. "La Solidaridad de Cuba con Angola." *America Latina* (Moscow) 21, 1: 113-29.

Krasner, Steven. 1978. *Defending the National Interest*. Princeton: Princeton University Press.

Krauthammer, Charles. 1985. "The Reagan Doctrine." *Time*, 1 April.

Kristol, Irving. 1985. "Foreign Policy in an Age of Ideology." *The National Interest* (Fall).

Kuhne, Winrich. 1985. "What Does the Case of Mozambique Tell Us about Soviet Ambivalence toward Africa?" *CSIS Africa Notes*, 30 August.

Lara, Lucio. 1963. Inaugural address to MPLA cadre school, Léopoldville (Kinshasa), February 1963. In *Vitoria ou morte*, 27 April.

Lefort, René. 1983. *Ethiopia, An Heretical Revolution*. London: Zed Press.

Legum, Colin. 1980. "African Outlooks toward the USSR." In Albright, ed.

_____. 1976. *After Angola.* New York: Africana.

_____. 1984. "The Soviet Union's Encounter with Africa." In Nation and Kauppi, eds.

_____. 1985. "Document Spells out Alleged Soviet Role in Ethiopia." *Christian Science Monitor,* 3 June.

Legvold, Robert. 1970. *Soviet Policy in West Africa.* Cambridge, Mass.: Harvard University Press, 1970.

_____. 1977. "The Nature of Soviet Power." *Foreign Affairs* (October).

_____. 1979. "The Super Rivals: Conflict in the Third World." *Foreign Affairs* (Spring).

LeoGrande, William. 1980. *Cuba's Policy in Africa, 1959-1980.* Berkeley: Institute of International Studies.

Luttwak, Edward. 1983. *The Grand Strategy of the Soviet Union.* New York: St. Martin's Press.

Makidi-Ku-Ntima. 1983. "On Struggle and the Making of the Revolution in Angola." *Contemporary Marxism,* no. 6 (Spring): 119-41.

Manchkha, Pyotr. 1983. *Problems of Africa Today.* Moscow: Progress Publishers.

Mangold, Peter. 1979. "Shaba I and Shaba II." *Survival* (May-June).

Marcum, John. 1969/1978. *The Angolan Revolution,* 2 vols. Cambridge, Mass.: MIT Press.

_____. 1985. "What the United States and the Soviet Union Have Learned in Twenty-Five Years of African Independence." Lecture delivered at the Africa Institute of South Africa, Pretoria, 4 October.

Moffa, Claudio. 1980. *La Rivoluzione etiopica, testi e documenti.* Urbino: Argalia Editore.

MPLA (Movimento Popular de Libertação de Angola). 1977. *Documentos e teses ao I Congresso.* Luanda: Jornal de Angola.

_____, Ministry of Information. 1976. *Documentos de independência.* Luanda.

_____. 1976. *Documentos: 3ª reunião plenaria do Comitê Central do MPLA.* Luanda.

_____. 1977. "Informação do Bureâu Político sobre a tentativa de golpe de 27 de maio." *Boletim do militante* (Luanda), 12 July.

MPLA-PT (Partido do Trabalho). 1985. *Declaration of the MPLA-PT on the Tenth Anniversary of the People's Republic of Angola.* In FBIS, 21 March 1985, p. U3.

Munslow, Barry. 1983. *Mozambique: The Revolution and Its Origins.* London: Longmans.

Nation, R. Craig, and Kauppi, Mark V., eds. 1984. *The Soviet Impact in Africa.* Lexington: Lexington Books.

Neto, Agostinho. 1979. *On Literature and National Culture*. Luanda: União dos Escritores Angolanos.

Neto, Antonio Alberto. 1967. "Contribution à l'étude du Mouvement Ouvrier Angolais dans le processus de la libération nationale." Mémoire de 2e cycle, University of Grenoble, October.

Nolutshungu, Sam. 1982. "African Interests and Soviet Power: The Local Context of Soviet Policy." *Soviet Studies* (July).

Ottaway, David, and Omang, Joane. 1985. "U.S. Course Uncharted on Aid to Insurgents." *Washington Post*, 27 May.

Ottaway, David, and Ottaway, Marina. 1978. *Ethiopia: Empire in Revolution*. New York: Africana.

_____, and _____. 1981. *Afrocommunism*. New York: Africana.

Ottaway, Marina. 1982. *Soviet and American Influence in the Horn of Africa*. New York: Praeger.

Oudes, Bruce, and Clough, Michael. 1978-79. "The United States's Year in Africa." *Africa Contemporary Record*.

Packenham, Robert. 1973. *Liberal America and the Third World*. Princeton: Princeton University Press.

Pearson, Roger, ed. 1977. *Sino-Soviet Intervention in Africa*. Washington, D.C.: Council on American Affairs.

Pipes, Richard. 1984. *Survival Is Not Enough*. New York: Simon and Schuster.

Podhoretz, Norman. 1976. "Making the World Safe for Communism." *Commentary* (April).

_____. 1980. "The Present Danger." *Commentary* (March).

_____. 1981. "The Future Danger." *Commentary* (April).

Porter, Bruce. 1984. *The USSR in Third World Conflicts*. Cambridge: Cambridge University Press.

PRA (People's Republic of Angola), Ministry of Information. 1976. *Documentos de independência*. Luanda.

Price, Robert. 1978. *U.S. Foreign Policy in Sub-Saharan Africa*. Berkeley: Institute of International Studies.

Radu, Michael. 1982. "Ideology, Parties, and Foreign Policy in Sub-Saharan Africa." *Orbis* (Winter).

Remek, Richard B. 1984. "Soviet Military Interests in Africa." *Orbis* (Spring): 123-43.

Republican Study Committee. 1985. "Missing Opportunities in Angola and Mozambique: The Failure of Constructive Engagement." 18 October.

Revel, Jean-Jacques. 1985. *How Democracies Perish*. New York: Perennial Library.

Roberts, Steven. 1985. "Some Paradoxes on What to Do about Angola." *New York Times*, 3 December.

Rosberg, Carl G., and Callaghy, Thomas, eds. 1979. *Socialism in Sub-Saharan Africa.* Berkeley: Institute of International Studies.

Rothchild, Donald, and Ravenhill, John. 1983. "From Carter to Reagan: The Global Perspective on Africa Becomes Ascendant." In *Eagle Defiant: United States Foreign Policy in the 1980s,* ed. Kenneth Oye et al., pp. 337-65. Boston: Little, Brown.

Rothenberg, Morris. 1980. *The USSR and Africa: New Dimensions of Soviet Global Power.* Miami: Advanced International Studies Institute.

Sada, Hugo. 1984. "Which African Policy?" *Jeune Afrique,* 22 February.

Saul, John. 1985. *A Difficult Road: The Transition to Socialism in Mozambique.* New York: Monthly Review Press.

Saunders, Gregory. 1983. "The Foreign Policy of Angola under Agostinho Neto." Master's thesis, Naval Postgraduate School (December).

Schwab, Peter. 1985. *Ethiopia—Politics, Economics and Society.* Boulder, Colo.: Lynne Rienner.

Selassie, Bereket. 1980. *Conflict and Intervention in the Horn of Africa.* New York: Monthly Review Press.

Shoemaker, Christopher, and Spanier, John. 1984. *Patron-Client State Relationships.* New York: Praeger.

Shulman, Marshall. 1973. "Toward a Western Philosophy of Coexistence." *Foreign Affairs* (October).

Sidenko, V. 1960. "The Last African Colonies: Angola." *New Times* (Moscow), no. 50 (December).

_____. 1961. *Angola v ogne.* Moscow: Polizdat.

Singleton, Seth. 1980. "Soviet Policy and Socialist Expansion in Asia and Africa." *Armed Forces and Society* (Spring).

_____. 1982. "The Natural Ally: Soviet Policy in Southern Africa." In *Changing Realities in Southern Africa,* ed. Michael Clough. Berkeley: Institute of International Studies.

Slovo, J. 1978. Interview with Lara in "Angola: Colonialismo e libertação." *Tempo* (Maputo), nos. 400, 401, 402.

Solarz, Steven. 1985. "It's Time for the Democrats to Be Tough-Minded." *New York Times,* 20 June.

Somerville, Keith. 1984. "The Soviet Union and Zimbabwe: The Liberation Struggle and After." In Nation and Kauppi, eds.

Stefansky, Stanley. 1985. "USSR Local War Doctrine as a Rationale for Development of the Soviet CTOL Aircraft Carrier." Master's thesis, Naval Postgraduate School (June).

Stevens, Christopher. 1976. *The Soviet Union and Black Africa.* New York: Holmes and Meier.

Thompson, Scott. 1980. "The African-American Nexus in Soviet Strategy." In Albright, ed.

LIST OF PUBLICATIONS (continued)

51. *Zionism and Territory.* Baruch Kimmerling. ($12.50)
52. *Soviet Subsidization of Trade with Eastern Europe.* M. Marrese & J. Vanous. ($14.50)
53. *Voluntary Efforts in Decentralized Management.* L. Ralston et al. ($9.00)
54. *Corporate State Ideologies.* Carl Landauer. ($5.95)
55. *Effects of Economic Reform in Yugoslavia.* John P. Burkett. ($9.50)
56. *The Drama of the Soviet 1960s.* Alexander Yanov. ($8.50)
57. *Revolutions and Rebellions in Afghanistan.* Eds. M. Nazif Shahrani & Robert L. Canfield. ($14.95)
58. *Women Farmers of Malawi.* D. Hirschmann & M. Vaughan. ($8.95)
59. *Chilean Agriculture under Military Rule.* Lovell S. Jarvis. ($11.50)
60. *Influencing Mass Political Behavior in the Netherlands and Austria.* Joseph J. Houska. ($11.50)

POLICY PAPERS IN INTERNATIONAL AFFAIRS

1. *Images of Detente & the Soviet Political Order.* K. Jowitt. ($1.25)
2. *Detente After Brezhnev: Domestic Roots of Soviet Policy.* A. Yanov. ($4.50)
3. *Mature Neighbor Policy: A New Policy for Latin America.* A. Fishlow. ($3.95)
4. *Five Images of Soviet Future: Review & Synthesis.* G.W. Breslauer. ($4.50)
5. *Global Evangelism: How to Protect Human Rights.* E.B. Haas. ($2.95)
6. *Israel & Jordan: An Adversarial Partnership.* Ian Lustick. ($2.00)
7. *Political Syncretism in Italy.* Giuseppe Di Palma. ($3.95)
8. *U.S. Foreign Policy in Sub-Saharan Africa.* Robert M. Price. ($4.50)
9. *East-West Technology Transfer in Perspective.* R.J. Carrick. ($5.50)
11. *Toward Africanized Policy for Southern Africa.* R. Libby. ($7.50)
12. *Taiwan Relations Act & Defense of ROC.* Edwin K. Snyder et al. ($7.50)
13. *Cuba's Policy in Africa, 1959-1980.* William M. LeoGrande. ($4.50)
14. *Norway, NATO, & Forgotten Soviet Challenge.* K. Amundsen. ($3.95)
15. *Japanese Industrial Policy.* Ira Magaziner and Thomas Hout. ($6.50)
16. *Containment, Soviet Behavior, & Grand Strategy.* Robert Osgood. ($5.50)
17. *U.S.-Japanese Competition-Semiconductor Industry.* M. Borrus et al. ($7.50)
18. *Contemporary Islamic Movements in Perspective.* Ira Lapidus. ($4.95)
19. *Atlantic Alliance, Nuclear Weapons, & European Attitudes.* W. Thies. ($4.50)
20. *War and Peace: Views from Moscow & Beijing.* B. Garrett & B. Glaser. ($7.95)
21. *Emerging Japanese Economic Influence in Africa.* Joanna Moss & John Ravenhill. ($8.95)
22. *Nuclear Waste Disposal under the Seabed.* Edward Miles et al. ($7.50)

POLITICS OF MODERNIZATION SERIES

1. *Spanish Bureaucratic-Patrimonialism in America.* M. Sarfatti. ($2.00)
2. *Civil-Military Relations in Argentina, Chile, & Peru.* L. North. ($2.00)
9. *Modernization & Bureaucratic-Authoritarianism: Studies in South American Politics.* Guillermo O'Donnell. ($8.95)

INSTITUTE OF INTERNATIONAL STUDIES
UNIVERSITY OF CALIFORNIA, BERKELEY

215 Moses Hall   Berkeley, California 94720

CARL G. ROSBERG, Director

Monographs published by the Institute include:

RESEARCH SERIES

1. *The Chinese Anarchist Movement.* R.A. Scalapino and G.T. Yu. ($1.00)
7. *Birth Rates in Latin America.* O. Andrew Collver. ($2.50)
16. *The International Imperatives of Technology.* Eugene B. Skolnikoff. ($2.95)
17. *Autonomy or Dependence in Regional Integration.* P.C. Schmitter. ($1.75)
19. *Entry of New Competitors in Yugoslav Market Socialism.* S.R. Sacks. ($2.50)
20. *Political Integration in French-Speaking Africa.* Abdul A. Jalloh. ($3.50)
21. *The Desert & the Sown: Nomads in Wider Society.* Ed. C. Nelson. ($5.50)
22. *U.S.-Japanese Competition in International Markets.* J.E. Roemer. ($3.95)
23. *Political Disaffection Among British University Students.* J. Citrin and D.J. Elkins. ($2.00)
24. *Urban Inequality and Housing Policy in Tanzania.* Richard E. Stren. ($2.95)
25. *The Obsolescence of Regional Integration Theory.* Ernst B. Haas. ($6.95)
26. *The Voluntary Service Agency in Israel.* Ralph M. Kramer. ($2.00)
27. *The SOCSIM Microsimulation Program.* E. A. Hammel et al. ($4.50)
28. *Authoritarian Politics in Communist Europe.* Ed. Andrew C. Janos. ($8.95)
30. *Plural Societies and New States.* Robert Jackson. ($2.00)
31. *Politics of Oil Pricing in the Middle East, 1970-75.* R.C. Weisberg. ($4.95)
32. *Agricultural Policy and Performance in Zambia.* Doris J. Dodge. ($4.95)
33. *Five Classy Computer Programs.* E.A. Hammel & R.Z. Deuel. ($3.75)
34. *Housing the Urban Poor in Africa.* Richard E. Stren. ($5.95)
35. *The Russian New Right: Right-Wing Ideologies in USSR.* A. Yanov. ($5.95)
36. *Social Change in Romania, 1860-1940.* Ed. Kenneth Jowitt. ($4.50)
37. *The Leninist Response to National Dependency.* Kenneth Jowitt. ($4.95)
38. *Socialism in Sub-Saharan Africa.* Eds. C. Rosberg & T. Callaghy. ($12.95)
39. *Tanzania's Ujamaa Villages: Rural Development Strategy.* D. McHenry. ($5.95)
40. *Who Gains from Deep Ocean Mining?* I.G. Bulkley. ($3.50)
41. *Industrialization & the Nation-State in Peru.* Frits Wils. ($5.95)
42. *Ideology, Public Opinion, & Welfare Policy.* R.M. Coughlin. ($6.50)
43. *The Apartheid Regime: Political Power and Racial Domination.* Eds. R.M. Price and C. G. Rosberg. ($12.50)
44. *Yugoslav Economic System in the 1970s.* Laura D. Tyson. ($5.95)
45. *Conflict in Chad.* Virginia Thompson & Richard Adloff. ($7.50)
46. *Conflict and Coexistence in Belgium.* Ed. Arend Lijphart. ($8.95)
47. *Changing Realities in Southern Africa.* Ed. Michael Clough. ($12.50)
48. *Nigerian Women Mobilized, 1900-1965.* Nina E. Mba. ($12.95)
49. *Institutions of Rural Development.* Eds. D. Leonard & D. Marshall. ($11.50)
50. *Politics of Women & Work in USSR & U.S.* Joel C. Moses. ($9.50)

United States, Department of Commerce. 1984. *Foreign Economic Trends and Their Implications for the United States: Mozambique* (July).

_____, House of Representatives, Committee on Foreign Affairs, African Affairs Subcommittee. 1985. Hearings (March).

Valenta, Jiri. 1980. "Soviet Decision-Making on the Intervention in Angola." In Albright, ed.

Valenta, Jiri, and Valenta, Virginia. 1984. "Leninism in Grenada." *Problems of Communism* (July-August).

Vance, Cyrus. 1983. *Hard Choices.* New York: Simon and Schuster.

Vanneman, Peter, and James, Martin. 1976. "Soviet Intervention in Angola." *Strategic Review* (Summer).

Walt, Steven. 1985. "Alliance Formation and the Balance of World Power." *International Security.*

Washington, Shirley. 1982. "Portugal's New Initiatives." *Africa Report* 27, 6 (November-December).

WCPD: RR. Weekly Compilation of Presidential Documents: Administration of Ronald Reagan.

White, Gordon. 1983. "What Is a Communist System?" *Studies in Comparative Communism* (Winter).

Wisner, Frank. 1984. "U.S. Normalizing Ties with Lusophone Africa." *Africa Wireless File,* No. 129 (3 July).

_____. 1985. "The United States, Portugal and Africa." Remarks to a conference on tripartite cooperation between the United States, Portugal, and Lusophone Africa; Lisbon (May).

Wolfers, Michael, and Bergerol, Jane. 1983. *Angola in the Frontline.* London: Zed Press.

Young, Crawford. 1982. *Ideology and Development in Africa.* New Haven: Yale University Press.

Zafris, Nicos. 1982. "The People's Republic of Angola." In *The New Communist Third World,* ed. Peter Wiles. New York: St. Martin's Press.

ISBN 0-87725-525-3

Although a likely arena for superpower opportunity and thus potential contention, sub-Saharan Africa may also be the region in which it will be easiest to work out modes of superpower crisis prevention, and in which a non-zero-sum relationship between the United States and USSR might evolve. As such, sub-Saharan Africa can serve as a unique laboratory for the study of U.S.-Soviet interaction.

From the FOREWORD